Ian Bradley is Emeritus Profess[...] History at the University of St An[...] are *Pilgrimage: A Cultural and Spiritual Journey* (2009), *Argyll: The Making of a Spiritual Landscape* (St Andrew Press, 2015), *Following the Celtic Way* (Darton, Longman & Todd, 2018) and *The Fife Pilgrim Way* (Birlinn, 2019).

The Coffin Roads: Journeys to the West is the second in a trilogy of books on aspects of death and the afterlife. The first, *The Quiet Haven: An Anthology of Readings on Death and Heaven*, was published in 2021 by Darton, Longman & Todd and the third, *Breathers of an Ampler Air: Heaven and the Victorians*, is due to be published by the Sacristy Press in 2024.

The Coffin Roads

Journeys to the West

Ian Bradley

BIRLINN

First published in 2022 by
Birlinn Limited
West Newington House
10 Newington Road
Edinburgh
EH9 1QS

www.birlinn.co.uk

ISBN: 978 1 78027 779 0

British Library Cataloguing-in-Publication Data

A catalogue record for this book is available from the British Library

Typeset by Initial Typesetting Services, Edinburgh

Papers used by Birlinn are from well-managed forests and
other responsible sources

Printed and bound by Clays Ltd, Elcograf S.p.A.

Contents

Acknowledgements

I have derived considerable benefit from conversations with Dr Lorn Macintyre, Alastair McIntosh, Iain Thornber, Lord Bruce Weir, Canon John Paul MacKinnon, Father William Fraser and Father Roddy Johnston. I am grateful to Iain Thomson for permission to quote from *Isolation Shepherd*, to Dr Mickey Vallee for permission to quote from the 1955 article by his grandfather, Professor Frank Vallee, on burial practices in Barra, and to John Bell and the Wild Goose Resource Group for permission to quote 'The Last Journey'. Hugh Andrew and Andrew Simmons of Birlinn have been consistently supportive and helpful. Helen Bleck has been a meticulous copy editor.

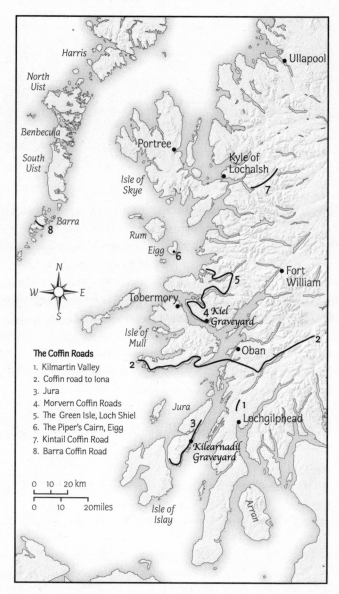

The Coffin Roads

1. Kilmartin Valley
2. Coffin road to Iona
3. Jura
4. Morvern Coffin Roads
5. The Green Isle, Loch Shiel
6. The Piper's Cairn, Eigg
7. Kintail Coffin Road
8. Barra Coffin Road

This map shows only the coffin roads and graveyards featured in the numbered chapters and not those mentioned in the Introduction

Introduction

Walkers and cyclists exploring the Highlands and Islands of Scotland are very likely to find that coffin roads feature on their itineraries alongside drovers' tracks and other traditional rights of way. Some of the most popular and well publicised walks in the west of Scotland carry this somewhat macabre designation. Perhaps the most frequented is the five-mile Stoneymollan coffin road from Balloch to Cardross, which forms part of both the John Muir Way and the Three Lochs Way, and links Loch Lomond with the Firth of Clyde.

Longer coffin roads are to be found rather further afield in the north-west Highlands. They include several challenging routes promoted on websites like ScotWays Heritage Paths and Walkhighlands, such as the nine-mile path from Kenmore to Applecross, the 26-mile Kintail coffin road from Glen Strathfarrar to the graveyard at Clachan Duich on the north shore of Loch Duich and the 28-mile Bunavullin coffin road which crosses Morvern from Bunavullin to Laudale House on Loch Sunart.

Another lengthy coffin road, which has been researched by the South Loch Ness Heritage Group, is thought to have extended for 25 miles from Whitebridge on the east side of Loch Ness to the burial ground at St Kenneth's Church at the north end of Loch Laggan. It went over the Monadhliath hills and through Glen Markie, crossed the Spey at Crathie and then passed Loch

Crunachdan before reaching its destination at Kinlochlaggan. Early Ordnance Survey maps show Cnocan nan Cisteachan to the west of Loch Crunachdan as 'the Hillock of the Coffins'. Shorter walks along coffin roads include the one-and-a-half mile Bohenie coffin road, which goes through Glen Roy from Bohenie to Achluachrach in Lochaber, the two-mile track along the north side of Loch Moidart from Glenuig to Kinlochmoidart, and the two-and-a-half mile track which climbs through native birch-wood from near Abriachan on the northern side of Loch Ness.

There are also numerous coffin roads on the islands of the Outer and Inner Hebrides, the best-known perhaps being the four-mile track that crosses the south of Harris from Leacklea (sometimes spelled as Lacklee or Leac-a-li) near the head of Loch Stockinish in the Bays area on the east of the island to Tràigh Losgaintir on the west. Known as the Bealach Eòrabhat, it stood in for the desolate landscape of Jupiter in Stanley Kubrick's 1968 film *2001: A Space Odyssey*, which included helicopter shots of the route. It also provides the title for Peter May's best-selling eco-thriller, *Coffin Road*, first published in 2016, which begins with the central protagonist being washed up ashore on Luskentyre beach (Tràigh Losgaintir) on the south-west coast of Harris. He has lost his memory and has no idea who he is or how he has come to be there. The only clue that he can find is a folded Ordnance Survey Explorer Map of South Harris, on which he has highlighted with a marker pen the route of the Bealach Eòrabhat. So it is on that coffin road that he begins the search for his lost identity. There are well-attested coffin roads on Mull and Barra.

As their name implies, these ancient and well-worn tracks were developed so that the bodies of the dead could be carried for burial to the remote graveyards that are still such a feature of the West Highland and Hebridean landscapes. They tended to be specially designated for this purpose, and to be distinct from routes along which the living would pass on their daily business, although several were later adopted as public tracks and roads. Journeys along the coffin roads were often lengthy and arduous, with relays of six or eight men carrying the coffin either on their shoulders or on long spokes. They would stop at frequent intervals for rest and refreshment and to be relieved by another bearer party. The slow progress on foot from place of death to place of burial could sometimes last for two or three days and nights and involve several hundred bearers and mourners walking through wild and desolate country with their food, drink and bedding carried by packhorses.

Along the routes of many of the coffin roads, cairns were erected, as illustrated on the front cover of this book. Some of them can still be seen today. They marked the places where the bearer parties stopped to rest. In some cases, the cairns may even have provided a platform on which the coffin was rested. Those carrying coffins would either build a small cairn to commemorate the dead at each resting place or add stones to an existing cairn along the route so that the 'resting cairns' gradually grew in size. Perhaps the most spectacular ones that can still be seen today are the four prominent cairns on Dun Scobull on the Ardmeanach peninsula on southeast Mull, which mark the place where the coffins of successive generations of the MacGillivray family were rested on their way to be buried at Kilfinchen churchyard. On his travels through the Highlands in 1927, Thomas Ratcliffe Barnett saw several heaps of coffins on the Glensherra road between Loch Crunachdan and Loch Laggan. I have not myself been able to verify if they are still visible today, but I have seen small heaps of stones beside the old coffin road along the south side of the Morvern peninsula between Fiunary and the graveyard at Kiel Church (see pp. 66–7).

The placing of cairns at stopping places along the routes of coffin roads was a ritual charged with deep significance and involved a much more deliberate and solemn action than the modern practice of walkers and climbers adding a stone to the cairn at the top of a mountain. Its importance was noted by Norman MacLeod, the mid nineteenth-century Church of Scotland minister whose *Reminiscences of a Highland Parish* provide rich source material for this book: 'When the body, on the day of funeral, is carried a considerable distance, a cairn of stones is always raised on the spots where the coffin has rested, and this cairn is from time to time renewed by friends and relatives. Hence the Gaelic saying or prayer with reference to the departed, "Peace to thy soul, and a stone to thy cairn!" thus expressing the wish that the remembrance of the dead may be cherished by the living.'[1]

The coffin roads which criss-cross the Highlands and Islands come in all shapes and sizes. Some are relatively short and simple, connecting a township with its nearest graveyard. Others are much longer and more complex, involving crossings of lochs and the sea, as in the routes by which coffins were taken for burial on Iona, which involved both long overland walks and one or more journeys by boat. The places at which coffins were loaded onto boats and unloaded were often called either *port nam marbh* (the port of the dead) or *carraig nam marbh* (the rock of the dead), from the Gaelic word *marbh* meaning a dead person or corpse. Port nam Marbh is found as a placename on the north-east coast of Islay, on the south-west side of the Kintyre peninsula just north of Campbeltown Airport, near Kilchoan on the Ardnamurchan peninsula and near Castlebay on Barra. Carraig nam Marbh near Kilninver on Loch Feochan is where coffins brought via several routes across the mainland were loaded onto boats for passage to Iona, some travelling there directly and being landed at Port nam Mairtear (now known as Martyrs' Bay), others going via Mull, where they were unloaded at Port nam Marbh on the northern side of the entrance to Loch Spelve.

There is one striking characteristic that most coffin roads have in common: they tend to go from east to west. There are practical, cultural and spiritual reasons for this. On islands like Harris, Barra and Eigg, the east coast was often too rocky and barren for any grave to be dug and so those who died there had to be taken for burial in graveyards on the west coast machair, with its deep and easily dug sandy soil. Graveyards were often sited near a loch or on the edge of the Atlantic Ocean, for reasons that will be explored later in this book, with bodies being taken to them from the more inland easterly regions. Highland and Hebridean people desired if possible to die and certainly to be buried in the west, the place of the setting sun. They were by no means unusual in having this desire. There was a widespread belief in many early cultures and civilisations that the abode of the dead lay beyond the setting sun in some place far off to the west. In Homer's *Iliad* it was described as being situated in the far west beyond the River Oceanus which was thought to encircle the earth. Celtic mythology shared the Ancient Greek idea of islands of the blessed, heavenly realms lying far out in the western seas. These were the perceived location of the next world, variously described in Gaelic as Tír na nÓg (the land of eternal youth), Tír na mBeo (the land of the living), Tír fo Thuinn (the land under the waves) and Tír Tairngire (the promised land) and seen as lying beyond the setting sun far out in the western sea. Christianity did not dispel this notion, as popular stories like the Voyage of St Brendan testify, and the Hebridean islands continued to be favourite places to be buried throughout and beyond the Middle Ages, with Iona being pre-eminent among them. The body's final journey, like that of the soul, was more often than not a journey to the west.

Numerous superstitions attached to the coffin roads and many stories centred on them. There was a belief among some

Highlanders that if the coffin touched the ground, the spirit of the deceased would return to haunt the living. For this reason, coffins would be rested on the cairns erected at stopping places. Coffins were generally carried with the corpse's feet facing away from home to avoid the possibility of the spirit returning to haunt it, and coffin bearers took care not to step off the path onto neighbouring farmland lest the crops should be blighted. The somewhat circuitous and meandering route taken by some coffin roads was sometimes explained by a desire to frustrate spirits, which were known to like to travel in straight lines, and a similar reason was given for their propensity to cross running water, something that spirits were thought unable to do. Coffin roads were commonly associated with premonitions and omens of death, known in Gaelic as *manadh air bàs*. Those gifted with second sight had premonitions of ghostly funeral processions along them which proved to be accurate predictions of future deaths. There is at least one well-documented instance of a walker traversing what had previously been a coffin road and experiencing a frightening and graphic vision of a bloody massacre which he described as a 'backward glimpse into a blood-stained page of Highland history' (see pp. 118–19). There are also stories of people being carried in coffins when they were still alive. One such involves a funeral procession along the Harris coffin road. When the bearers stopped for a rest, they heard a noise from inside the coffin. They opened it and found that the person inside was still alive, so she was carried back to the east coast. These and other stories and superstitions are the subject of Chapter 7.

There are some wonderfully detailed and evocative accounts of funeral processions along Highland and Hebridean coffin roads, most of them dating from the nineteenth century, which was perhaps their heyday, although they were in existence long before then and some continued to be used into the early years of the twentieth century. Several of these accounts will feature in the pages that follow, but to give an early taste of what journeys along a coffin road could be like, here are the recollections of Dr John Mackenzie, doctor and factor at Gairloch, of two contrasting funeral processions in which a coffin was carried many miles through the remote north-west Highlands in the early 1830s. The first was conducted 'in the old, old way, with whisky flowing like water'. The laird of Dundonnell had died in Edinburgh. His body was taken by sea to Inverness and then by horse and cart to Garve, where the road ended.

> At that spot it was met one evening by the whole of the adult male population of the Dundonnell estate. They were to start carrying the corpse early the following morning. There was no place where even a twentieth part of this crowd could sleep, so they all sat up through the whole of the night drinking themselves drunk, as there was any amount of drink provided for them, though probably but little food! Early in the morning a start was made by the rough track – the Diridh Mor – which led to Dundonnell, some twenty-five miles away. The crowd of semi-drunken men had marched several miles of the way, when one of the mourners, who was rather more sober than the rest, suddenly recollected that they had no coffin with them, they having left it behind them at Garve, and so back they all had to trudge to fetch their beloved laird.[2]

The other procession recalled by John Mackenzie was planned with military precision and could not have been more different. It involved the conveyance of the body of Lady Kythé Mackenzie, who had died in childbirth at the age of 23 in Gairloch where her husband was laird, for burial at Beauly Priory more than 70 miles away. In the absence of roads suitable for wheeled vehicles, Dr Mackenzie himself, acting in his capacity as the deceased's brother-in-law, resolved that the coffin should be carried shoulder-high by parties of men from the estate and the parish. He selected 500 men from more than a thousand volunteers for the task, which involved three days walking with the coffin and then three days walking back and so the loss of a week's work and wages.

> I picked out four companies of one hundred and twenty-five strong men, made them choose their four captains, and explained clearly to them all the arrangements. I was to walk at the coffin foot and Frank [Lady Kythé's husband] at the head all the way to Beauly, resting the first night at Kenlochewe and the next night at Conon, say twenty-four miles the first day and forty the second; the third day we were to reach Beauly and return to Conon, say nine miles. I sized the companies equally, the men in one company being all above six feet, and the others down to five feet nine or so. I had a bier made so that its side-rails should lie easily on the bearers' shoulders, allowing them to slip in and out of harness without any trouble or shaking of the coffin. We started with eight men of No. 1 company at the rear going to work, four on each side; the captain observed the proper time to make them fall out, when the eight next in front of them took their place, and so on till all the one hundred and twenty-five had taken their turn. Before all the men in No. 1 company were used up, the second company had divided, and the fresh bearers were all in front ready to begin their supplies of eight; the first

company filing back to be the rear company. Thus all had exactly their right share of the duty.

Had the men been drilled at the Guards Barracks in London, it would have been impossible for them to have gone through their willing task more perfectly and solemnly. Not one word was audible among the company on duty, or, indeed, in the other three; every sound was uttered sotto voce in the true spirit of mourning, and I am sure every man of them felt highly honoured by the service entrusted to him. All of us being good walkers, we covered, once we fairly started, about four miles an hour. With the help of Rory Mackenzie, the grieve at Conon, and James Kennedy, gardener and forester at Gairloch, we had prepared plenty of food for the five hundred before we started; the food was carried in creels on led horses for each halt on the way. We had plenty of straw or hay for beds at night, and charming weather all the way.

I doubt if ever a more silent, solemn procession than ours was seen or heard of, and, though it was nearly fifty years ago, I never can think of that wonderfully solemn scene with dry eyes. On the second day, some distance east of Achnasheen, we halted to give the men a little rest and some food. And as I spread them out on the sloping grassy braes above the road and saw food handed round by the captains, it was difficult not to think of the Redeemer when He miraculously fed the thousands who came to Him in a wilderness probably not very unlike the bleak Achnasheen moor. Before we moved away again every man had added a stone to the cairn on the spot where the coffin had rested.

Among those five hundred surely there were some not faultless in head or heart, yet sure I am that had more than a word of kindly thanks been offered to any one for his loss of a week's work and about one hundred and forty miles of most fatiguing walking, it would have fared ill with the offerer. Every man was there with his heart aching sadly for us. All were substantially and well dressed in their sailor homespun blue clothes, such as they may be seen wearing going to or returning from the herring-fishing. They were all dressed alike and quite sufficiently sombre for mourners; not a rag of moleskin or a patched knee or elbow was visible; all were in their Sunday-best clothes.[3]

Those two accounts reflect the very different ways in which death was approached by Highlanders. For some, it was an occasion for irreverent revelry and drunkenness, both during the wake that followed immediately after someone died and at the funeral. For others it was a matter of the utmost solemnity. These two responses could co-exist at the same time, as evidenced in some of the other accounts of funerals which will appear later in this book. They point to the mixture of ritual, respect, emotion and excess which surrounded death in the Highlands and the Hebrides. John Mackenzie's recollections also point to the huge number of people who took part in Highland funerals and the processions along the coffin roads. These were major public occasions which involved the whole community and which were remembered for years afterwards, becoming the subject of numerous stories and legends.

The ubiquity and the significance of the coffin roads provide an eloquent testimony to several key features of West Highland and Hebridean culture and religion. Perhaps the most striking, still evident today, is the desire to be buried among one's ancestors and in the place where family members had rested for generations. Those born in the Highlands and Islands often left home and travelled far away to seek their fortunes, not returning to their place of birth in their lifetimes. In death, however, they were determined to return and it was their last journey along the coffin road that brought them home. This characteristic was eloquently described by Norman MacLeod:

> The Celt has a strong desire, almost amounting to a decided superstition, to lie beside his kindred. He is intensely social in his love of family and tribe. It is long ere he takes to a stranger as bone of his bone and flesh of his flesh. When sick in the distant hospital, he will, though years have separated him from home and trained him to be a citizen of the world, yet dream in his delirium of the old burial-ground. To him there is in this idea a sort of homely feeling, a sense of friendship, a desire for a congenial neighbourhood, that, without growing into a belief of which he would be ashamed, unmistakably circulates as an instinct in his blood, and cannot easily be dispelled. It is thus that the poorest Highlanders always endeavour to bury their dead with kindred dust. The pauper will save his last penny to secure this boon.[4]

The desire to be buried among one's ancestors in the consecrated ground of a graveyard was reinforced by a widespread belief in the Christian doctrine of a day of resurrection when the dead would rise from their tombs and assume new bodies to enter the new heaven and new earth promised in the biblical Book of Revelation. This meant that it was important that the whole body was laid to rest in the graveyard with no parts left missing. Among the stories about the coffin roads of the north-west Highlands collected by Archibald Robertson, a Church of Scotland minister who was the chairman of the Scottish Rights of Way Society and is generally regarded as the first person to have climbed all 282 Scottish Munros, was one about an unusual journey made in 1894 on the track from Glen Garry to Glen Moriston. An inhabitant of Glen Moriston had been staying in Invergarry when he had an accident which necessitated the amputation of his leg. 'His brother came across and carried the leg over Ceann a' Mhaim and buried it in the old graveyard where they would all one day rest. This shows what store the old Highlanders laid on their being buried, as far as possible, whole and intact, so that at the resurrection they would arise perfect and entire.'[5]

The involvement of family members – in this case, a brother – is significant here. In most Highland and Island funerals, it was members of the family of the deceased who undertook all aspects of the mourning rituals and preparation for the funeral. They hosted and provided refreshments for the wake, and organised and supervised the carrying of the coffin, as Dr John Mackenzie did for his sister-in-law, and the digging of the grave, which was often undertaken by neighbours and friends. They also generally presided at the burial, which was usually conducted without the presence of a clergyman, almost invariably so in Protestant communities.

The often long and arduous procession along the coffin road by which the deceased was taken home, carried and accompanied by family members and by many if not all of the local community, symbolised and underlined the idea of death as a journey. The passage from this life to the next was seen as a gradual rather than an instant process and marked by a series of rituals. Death was, indeed, prepared for well in advance, with young brides regarding one of their first duties after marriage as being to prepare winding sheets for their own and their husband's interments. When someone was clearly near death, they were visited, tended and ministered to not just by family members but also by friends and neighbours. Semi-professional mourning women might be brought in to sing the death croon over them and ease their passage into the next world. After death, the body was washed and dressed and left lying prominently in the front room of the house, often with a plate of salt placed on the breast. From the time of death until the interment, which was usually a period of two days and nights, the body was constantly watched over by a family member, with a wake held in the house to which all friends and neighbours would be invited and which often became raucous and exuberant. Once the grave had been dug and the mourners assembled, the funeral procession set off along the coffin road to the graveyard. After the interment, all those present were liberally entertained with drink and food, first around the graveside and then later at some local hostelry or specially erected tent, or if the weather allowed it, in the open air.

These rituals, which will be described in more detail in later chapters, played a key role in easing and facilitating the grieving process. They provided numerous tasks, some of them backbreaking like the digging of the grave and the carrying of the coffin, which occupied people and gave them a purpose and a focus at a time of emotional upset and sorrow. They punctuated the period following death with familiar, reassuring domestic and community activities and created a kind of liminal or threshold space which blurred the hard edges between living and dying and gently eased both the deceased and the mourners into their changed state.

The coffin roads are just part of a wider landscape of death which cannot but strike modern visitors to the Highlands and Islands. Even more ubiquitous and certainly more visible today are the many graveyards and cemeteries scattered across the region which were the destinations of the coffin roads. They are often sited in seemingly very remote places, high up on the slopes of hills or down on the side of a loch or a quiet seashore, sometimes protected from the wind by trees and nearly always surrounded by stone walls. Some are very ancient and virtually inaccessible, like Cladh a' Bhile at Ellary by Loch Caolisport in mid-Argyll, which has nearly 30 cross-marked stones dating from the seventh and eighth centuries. Many are overgrown, often with the crumbling ruins of a small chapel in their midst, while others are still very much in use and well-tended. Within them, small worn stones decorated with no more than a simple incised cross stand side by side with elaborately carved grave slabs bearing the effigies of soldiers and prelates and massive mausoleums, burial aisles and enclosures erected to house the bodies of the rich and well-to-do, more often than not Campbells.

These graveyards have become important places of pilgrimage. People come from all over the world to visit them in order to trace their ancestors, thanks partly to the growing fascination with family trees and genealogy. Indeed, they have become among the most visited parts of the Highland and Hebridean landscape. Many people enjoy walking around them simply because of their atmosphere and the interesting artwork and inscriptions on their gravestones. We feel a sense of timeless peace and tranquillity as we walk among the ancient lichen-covered tombs which have taken on the character of works of art or historical monuments. Those who erected and engraved them saw them in a very different light. Often marking tragically early diseased and violent deaths, their prime purpose was to remind those still alive of the frailty of our human clay and the reality of mortality. This is why more than anywhere else in the British Isles, the graveyards of the West Highlands and the Hebrides are full of stones engraved with trumpets, hourglasses, skulls and crossbones with their inescapable message, sometimes spelled out explicitly in inscriptions beside these symbols of mortality, *memento mori* – remember you must die.

Just as with the coffin roads, various superstitions attached to these graveyards. There was a widespread belief that the last person to be buried had to keep watch and look after all those resting there until the next interment took place. This was regarded as an onerous responsibility and on occasions when two burials took place on the same day it was not unusual for each group of mourners to make great efforts, including resorting to physical force, to make sure that they reached the graveyard first so that their loved one was not left with the task of looking after the dead (see p. 74). The sense that the dead are waiting in the graveyard for their families and descendants to join them lingered well into the twentieth century. An old woman in Skye, who was a loyal member of the Church of Scotland, told the Gaelic scholar John MacInnes shortly before her death in the late 1950s that she believed the dead lie waiting in the cemetery 'longing until the last of the future generations should join them, whereupon their society would be complete'.[6]

For those aware of these beliefs and traditions, and of the Christian teaching that our condition post-mortem is one of a long sleep until the Day of Resurrection, walking the coffin roads and visiting the graveyards of the Highlands and Islands today may perhaps induce a sense of the lingering presence of the dead. Do they indeed continue in some way to inhabit the physical landscape? This has been suggested in a very interesting way by the Irish theologian Noel Dermot O'Donoghue, who lectured in the Faculty of Divinity at the University of Edinburgh in the 1970s and 1980s, the first Roman Catholic to do so since the Reformation. In his book *The Mountain Behind the Mountain: Aspects of the Celtic Tradition* he writes about the churchyard in Ireland where his parents were buried:

This is the elemental earth from which I came, as they, my forefathers and mothers, came and to which I too shall return. In a sense these people are not where their bones lie; they are elsewhere, as I too shall be as they place my remains in the element of the earth or the element of fire. Yet the funeral rite speaks of the resurrection of the body as if the whole person somehow awaited resurrection here in this place. There is an ambiguity here that Christian theology, from the time of Saint Augustine until today, has never quite resolved. Are the dead alive in another region, or do they somehow, somewhere *await* an awakening? Are they still somehow part of nature, or do they dwell in a spirit world which may be near to us but is yet of a totally different substance?[7]

O'Donoghue points to the way that in folk consciousness the dead are regarded as a lingering presence in the physical landscape, as suggested by such phrases as 'the good dead in the green hills' or 'she is gone to her people'. He quotes Lord Byron recalling his own ancestry in a wild Highland place:

Clouds there encircle the forms of our fathers;
They dwell in the tempests of dark Lochnagar.

O'Donoghue also quotes the great twentieth-century Jesuit theologian, Karl Rahner, who wrote in his book *On the Theology of Death*: 'we cannot rule out the possibility that in death the relationship which we have with the world is not abolished, but is rather, for the first time, completed . . . through death the soul becomes not a-cosmic but all-cosmic'.[8]

I will come back to these deep spiritual matters later in this book, just as I will also reflect on the way that Hebrideans and

Highlanders, like so many Christians, held both to the doctrine of the resurrection of the dead and also to the idea of the immortality of the soul, with its suggestion that on death we do not go to sleep but are released and freed from our bodies and go to another world; in Christian terms, heaven, or perhaps purgatory. But for the moment let us notice the sense of closeness between the spiritual and the physical and the close relationship of humans to the natural landscape and the rest of creation that is expressed by the coffin roads and the graveyards. They point to death as being something natural and part of the rhythm and cycle of life. The bodies of the dead return to the earth after their last journey over the hills and across lochs and seas. Their souls perhaps escape down the streams that are almost invariably found beside graveyards to merge in the great ocean of divine love and find rest in the islands of the blessed far out in the west beyond the setting sun.

Ultimately, what the coffin roads and the rituals and beliefs that surrounded them testify to most eloquently is an approach to death and dying that was open, holistic, public and deeply healthy. It is a world away from our modern approach where people mostly die in hospital side rooms, their bodies are whisked away by an undertaker, sealed in a coffin and, after a period where they lie usually alone and unvisited in a refrigerator or embalmed in a funeral parlour, are transported by hearse to a crematorium where they are incinerated in a gas oven.

The traditional Hebridean and Highland way of death could not be more different. Virtually everyone died at home, accompanied on their pilgrimage to the next world by family members as well as by a minister or priest. After death, their bodies lay at home so that friends and neighbours could visit them, say their farewells and often share a joke and a reminiscence, before the final journey along the coffin road to their resting place in

the graveyard. Instead of the impersonality, privacy and con-
veyor-belt-like quality of the modern cremation and funeral
industry, here was something deeply personal, communal and
public, where there was celebration and thanksgiving as well as
mourning and keening, and none of the hushing up, the embar-
rassed avoidance of the topic and of the bereaved that so often
surrounds death today.

After more than a century when the subject has been largely
taboo, death is at last being widely discussed, confronted and
even embraced. Even before the Covid pandemic brought it daily
into every television news bulletin and onto every front page,
there were already significant figures in the medical profession
questioning whether we have become too concerned with pro-
longing life at whatever cost and regardless of its quality. There
is increasing public interest and debate around issues of assisted
dying and the rise of the death café movement across Britain and
beyond has shown that a large number of people want to talk
about death and what may lie beyond it and that long-held inhi-
bitions around the subject are finally disappearing.

In the context of this new interest and openness about death
and the afterlife, it seems appropriate to revisit some of the beliefs
and traditions held by our ancestors who were very much less
reticent and inhibited about confronting and even embracing
these subjects than we are. I believe that the approach to dying
and death of those living in the Highlands of Scotland, especially
the West Highlands, and in the Hebridean islands from pre-
Christian times to the early twentieth century may well have
much to teach us today, and that is why I have written this book.

My approach in the chapters that follow is largely chron-
ological. We begin with the prehistoric period and end in the
mid twentieth century, which is when the distinctive practices

were beginning to die out, although some still remain. There is a predominance of material drawn from the nineteenth century, which was when the coffin roads were being written about by a number of very perceptive and illuminating chroniclers and folklore collectors, and perhaps when they were most in use. The book also has a geographical trajectory, moving broadly from south to north.

I focus on eight coffin roads and their destinations, with each prompting wider reflections on a particular aspect of the Highland and Hebridean approach to death. Chapter 1 describes the Kilmartin Valley in mid-Argyll as the archetypal coffin road and looks at its importance as a landscape populated by the dead and its use of stone to commemorate them. Chapter 2 takes the Street of the Dead on Iona as a way into exploring Celtic Christian beliefs about death and dying. Chapter 3 begins in the graveyards of Jura and provides accounts of funerals there and in other places in the early nineteenth century. Chapter 4 starts with the coffin roads of Morvern, which lead to the cemetery at Kiel Church about which Norman MacLeod wrote so eloquently and interestingly. Chapter 5 explores what is often regarded as the oldest graveyard in continuous use anywhere in Europe, the Green Isle on Loch Shiel, and considers the importance of islands as burial places and the striking prevalence of symbols and inscriptions imparting the stark message of *memento mori* on West Highland grave slabs. In Chapter 6 the Piper's Cairn on the Eigg coffin road prompts a discussion of the songs, death croons and laments associated with Highland and Hebridean funerals and collected at the end of the nineteenth century by Alexander Carmichael and Kenneth Macleod. Chapter 7 begins with the unnerving experience of a walker on the old Kintail coffin road and goes on to explore premonitions and omens of death associated especially with the possession of second sight. Chapter 8 is set on Barra and draws heavily on accounts of death and funeral practices there in the mid twentieth century. The Epilogue summarises the distinctive approach to death, dying and the afterlife which has been found in the Highlands and the Hebrides and suggests that it can perhaps offer us helpful insights and ways of dealing with these difficult, frightening and disturbing realities today.

The Original Coffin Road
Kilmartin Valley

I have never seen Kilmartin Valley – near Lochgilphead in mid-Argyll – described as a coffin road but that is in fact exactly what it was, on a gigantic and unequalled scale. Indeed, it could well claim to be the archetypal coffin road. For more than 3,000 years, the bodies or cremated remains of the dead were carried through it on their way to burial. There are around 800 prehistoric monuments scattered along the valley floor and on the adjoining slopes, ranging from standing stones, burial cists and henges to incised rock faces, and forming the largest concentration of their kind anywhere in western Europe. Amid all these archaeological remains, there is virtually no evidence of any human settlement in terms of domestic dwellings, food remains or activities like metal-working. This has led archaeologists to suggest that the valley was probably deliberately laid out as a ritual funerary landscape and that no one actually lived there. It is, indeed, well described in the video shown at the Kilmartin House Museum as 'the valley of ghosts'.

This ritual landscape of the dead was laid out, adapted and reconfigured over a period of around 3,000 years between 4000 and 1000 BCE. The earliest clear archaeological evidence of human activity in the Kilmartin Valley comes from the later Neolithic period, around 4000 BCE. This was the time of transition in human evolution from nomadic hunter-gathering to the more settled activities of growing crops and tending animals. With this transition came a much greater sense of investment in place. People began clearing forests, planting crops and building homes. In the case of the Kilmartin Valley, this investment showed itself not in such domestic activities but rather in a new sense of the sacredness of place, expressed through the building of ritual funerary monuments. As the archaeologist Graham Ritchie has pointed out, Argyll's earliest agricultural communities left their mark on the landscape, not through fields or farms, but with the burial places of their dead.[1]

Among the earliest of the monuments built in the valley are thought to have been two parallel lines of timber posts erected along a 400-metre stretch of gravel terrace at Upper Largie, just half a mile north of Kilmartin village, which appear to date from around 3800 BCE. They have been variously interpreted as marking a ceremonial route through which bodies were carried on their way to burial, the first and grandest coffin road, or as delineating a boundary between the worlds of the living and the dead. Either way, they signal the beginning of a process by which the valley was laid out as a ritual landscape specifically associated with death. We will, of course, never know the precise nature of the rituals which took place within this designated sacred space, but later constructions make clear that the valley's primary function was as a place of burial and strongly suggest that part at least of its purpose was both to delineate and to connect the worlds of the living and the dead.

Other early monuments were certainly built to house the dead, like the 20 or more chambered cairns, which date from around 3700 BCE. Constructed out of large boulders, they were places of communal burial, where grave goods like pottery and tools were placed alongside cremated human remains. Around 3000 BCE two circles were erected at a site later known as Temple Wood near Slockavullin on the west side of the valley. Initially made out of wood, they were later rebuilt with stone. These do not seem originally to have been designed as burial places, although they were subsequently adapted for that purpose. Like the later standing stones erected in the valley, they were possibly designed to mark the positions of sun, moon and stars. This may also conceivably have been one of the functions of the 'cup and ring' markings found on exposed rock surfaces around the valley, which probably date from between 2900 and 2500 BCE and form the largest concentration of rock art in Europe.

A significant change took place in the ritual landscape of the Kilmartin Valley around 2500 BCE, during what is known as the Chalcolithic period, with a move from communal to individual graves. Rising wealth and status meant that certain prominent individuals were singled out for special treatment, with their cremated remains being interred separately rather than in the company of others. With the transition from Stone Age to Bronze Age, the arrival of metal weapons and implements probably facilitated the emergence of a military and commercial élite whose status was demonstrated through the construction of conspicuous individual funerary monuments. This may explain the building between 2500 and 1500 BCE of what is known as the linear cemetery, a line of seven cairns through the middle of the valley floor. The most northerly, Glebe Cairn, can clearly be seen from Kilmartin House Museum and the most southerly, Ri Cruin, has a name which suggests that it was the burial place of a king, although this is probably anachronistic. Each of these cairns consists of a cist, or box-like tomb, dug into the ground and sealed with a stone capping slab, with water-smoothed stones heaped over the top. As with the timber posts erected 1,500 or so years earlier, but this time on a larger scale, the intention in constructing these cairns spaced out down the valley floor seems to have been to create an ordered ritual landscape centred on the themes of death and burial.

The valley continued to be used as a place of burial throughout the Middle and Later Bronze Age. The two stone circles at Temple Wood were adapted for this purpose during the period between 2300 and 2000 BCE, with two cist graves covered by small cairns being constructed outside the north-east circle and a massive cist grave being built in the centre of the south-west circle. Sometime between 1450 and 1200 BCE new burial monuments, known as 'kerb cairns', were built to contain the ashes of cremated human remains. Also in this period a massive timber circle was constructed on the Upper Largie gravel terrace, and groups of standing stones were erected at Ballymeanoch and Nether Largie.

Kilmartin Valley provides no archaeological evidence of the worship of gods and goddesses, as one might expect at such a primal and important ritual site. Rather, the overwhelming sense that the modern visitor gains from wandering among its many prehistoric monuments is of reverence for ancestors, the significance attached to the rite of cremation and burial and the continuing remembrance and presence of the dead. This is, indeed, a landscape peopled by the dead. Even those monuments, such as the standing stones and circles, which would appear originally to have had more of an astrological purpose, built to mark or predict movements of sun and moon and perhaps even to provide an early calendar to help with planting crops, seem later to have been pressed into service as burial sites. Traces of cremated human bone, carbon-dated to between 1400 and 1050 BCE, have been found around the base of one of the Ballymeanoch standing stones. Indeed, it has been suggested that the standing stones in the valley were themselves primarily funereal rather than astrological in purpose. Eighteenth-century antiquarians took them to be early grave markers, possibly commemorating those who had fallen in conflict, and more recent archaeologists have postulated that they may have marked the boundaries of processional routes associated with either the disposal or com-memoration of the departed.

Sometime around 1000 BCE, during the period of transition from the Bronze Age to the Iron Age, ritual activity seems to have ceased in Kilmartin Valley. The erection of burial mounds and standing stones gave way to the building of hill forts and duns, small defensive hilltop structures with disproportionately thick walls. Suggestions put forward to explain this dramatic change in the human-made landscape include the theory that the coming of iron weapons produced a more aggressive society focused on defending territory rather than remembering the dead. Whatever the reason, the valley became a place where the emphasis was no longer on honouring dead ancestors but rather on protecting the living. Rachel Butter calls it 'a tense landscape . . . now not known by reference to gods and ancestors but by reference to living political leaders and petty tyrants'.[2]

The archetypal coffin road created by the landscaping and layout of the Kilmartin Valley introduces several of the distinc-tive themes that have characterised the Highland and Hebridean approach to death and which will be explored further in the pages that follow. It suggests a veneration and remembrance of the dead, a conscious decision not to shut them away out of sight and out of mind but to locate their remains conspicuously, prom-inently and publicly. The processional routes marked out by the timber posts and the carefully constructed burial chambers and cists point to elaborate rituals surrounding cremation and inter-ment. Death was not treated casually or swept under the carpet but marked with considerable ceremony and reverence. As Isabel

Grant, who founded the Highland Folk Museum in Kingussie, observed more than 60 years ago in her book *Highland Folk Ways*: 'The ceremonies connected with death played a most important part in the old social life of the Highland people, and for that matter they do so still. It is tempting to wonder if this attitude of mind goes right back to our remote ancestors who built the megalithic tombs.'[3]

Although we have no literary evidence of what the prehistoric inhabitants of the Highlands and Islands believed about death and dying, we can make some suppositions about their attitudes from the archaeological remains that they left. The placing in graves of objects such as tools, weapons and pots, dishes and jugs, probably containing food and drink, suggests a belief in some kind of survival after death. Indeed, the world of the dead was probably assumed to be much like that of the living, with similar customs, occupations and hierarchies. This was a belief shared by several early indigenous peoples, including Australian aboriginals, the Inuit and related hunting tribes from the Arctic regions.

Perhaps the most striking aspect of the layout of the Kilmartin Valley as a carefully and purposefully constructed landscape of the dead is the use of stone to commemorate the deceased and mark the place where they have been laid to rest. Once again, of course, this is not a practice peculiar to this part of the world. Many ancient cultures and civilisations built great stone tombs to house their dead, most famously the Egyptians with the pyramids at Giza built between 2600 and 2200 BCE during the period known as the 'Old Kingdom'. There are bigger concentrations of gravestones in other parts of the world. The Wadi-us-Salaam (Valley of Peace) beside the Imam Ali mosque on the banks of the Euphrates in the town of Najaf in Iraq extends across 2.3 square miles and is believed to contain around 5 million gravestones. But there are few places which have quite the variety of different stone-built and shaped memorials to the dead as the Kilmartin Valley, ranging from henges, cists and cairns to standing stones and incised rocks. With its durability and permanence, stone is an obvious material to use to express a sense of immortality and long-lasting memory. Scotland has some of the oldest, hardest-wearing and most enduring rocks on Earth, formed over 2,800 million years ago, and they are predominantly found in the Highlands and Islands. It was while staying in Lochbuie on Mull during his tour of the Highlands and Islands that Dr Johnson made his famous observation to his Scottish host that 'Your country consists of two things, stone and water. There is, indeed, a little earth above the stone in some places, but a very little; and the stone is always appearing. It is like a man in rags; the naked skin is still peeping out.'[4]

The stone and rock which are so marked a feature of the geology of the region have been hugely important in commemorating the dead and establishing them as a continuing and visible presence in the landscape. It is possible to trace a direct line from the burial cists and standing stones of the Kilmartin Valley through the simple early Christian incised gravestones of Cladh a' Bhile and the highly decorated later medieval grave slabs now gathered together in places like Kilmartin churchyard to modern memorials in the shape of the ubiquitous ringed Celtic crosses found in cemeteries across Scotland. All are fashioned out of hard stone and granite and tend to support Isabel Grant's suggestion of the continuation of a practice, and, indeed, an attitude of mind, that goes back to those who built the megalithic tombs in mid-Argyll.

There is one very specific and enduring legacy that has survived from the layout of Kilmartin Valley as a conscious ritual landscape of the dead. It is the way that graves and tombs were constructed in the form of cairns by the heaping of stones and boulders one on top of another. This is very evident in many

of the valley's largest and most impressive monuments, such as
the Nether Largie chambered cairn, the Ballymeanoch henge
and the Temple Wood stone circle. These surely are the origins of
the cairns which played such a significant part in Highland and
Hebridean burial rituals, not just along the coffin roads but also
in the construction of graves and indeed in the way that funerals
were conceived and described. Their significance was noted by
Lord Teignmouth in his account of his travels through 'the coasts
and islands of Scotland' in the late 1820s:

> There is a Gaelic phrase signifying, 'If I be alive after
> your death, I will carefully lay a stone on your cairn'.
> The solemnities of burial are called in the Gaelic,
> *Toiradh*, i.e. the heaping of stones, the making of
> the cairn over the dead: the very word still used for a
> funeral. The invitation for a funeral, in literal terms, is
> to come and heap the cairn over such and such a person.
> The cairns or heaps of stones in the form of a cone, and
> other sepulchral remains, are traditionally reported to
> have been piled up for the purpose of protecting the
> bodies which they covered from the voracity of wolves,
> which abounded once in Scotland.[5]

Once again, it is worth noting that the practice of piling a heap
of stones, or cairn, on the graves of the dead was not peculiar to
the prehistoric inhabitants of the West Highlands. It was almost
certainly a feature of the Neolithic Age as a whole. Writing in his
historical study *Images of Afterlife* about the difficulty in discerning
attitudes towards death in this period, Geddes MacGregor comments: 'From practices in underdeveloped countries today we
may find hints that point us in the right direction. The practice
of piling a heap of stones on a grave and, in some African tribes,

a pile of thorns, provides a clue. It reflects a certain fear that the dead may come back to haunt the living. Such monuments may be construed as impeding them.'[6]

If it was, indeed, to prevent the dead coming back rather than to protect their corpses from wolves that the Neolithic peoples of the West Highlands built their substantial chambered cairns, we are brought back to the question raised in the Introduction as to how far the spirits of the deceased continued to haunt the living, and more broadly to what extent the dead remained a presence in the landscape. It may be that those who constructed the huge roomy tombs in the Kilmartin Valley consciously wished to maintain contact and communication with the dead. In their book *Inside the Neolithic Mind*, David Lewis-Williams and David Pearce suggest that what we call megalithic tombs were in fact something more than this: 'They were also places where the dead were revisited and where people maintained long-term relations with them: they were religious and social foci.'[7]

The coming of Christianity did much to dispel fears about spirits of the dead escaping from graves and haunting the living, and it may well be that this is why heavy solid chamber tombs of the kind found in the Kilmartin Valley gave way to much simpler and smaller gravestones. However, the sense of the dead remaining as a presence in the landscape continued and was remarked on by visitors to the West Highlands until relatively recent times. It was something that the United Free Church minister Thomas Ratcliffe Barnett frequently alluded to in his books and articles chronicling the walking tours through the region in the 1920s and 1930s, which he had initially taken up to provide therapeutic relief from the stress of ministering to shell-shocked soldiers at Craiglockhart Hospital in Edinburgh during the First World War. He felt it particularly in Argyll, where he noted the prevalence of graveyards, or God's Acres as he called them, and wrote that 'from end to end the whole of Argyll is strewn with castles of the dead'. He acknowledged that there were certain places where he felt a sense of the presence of the dead particularly acutely: 'I never loiter in Appin but I keep looking over my shoulder. For there is still an aura of ghosts about its glens and hills and a feeling along its shores that the dead are watching to see if the living are ever going to redd up some old scores that have never been settled.'[8]

A walk through Kilmartin Valley today can still induce a similar feeling. The video shown to visitors to the Kilmartin House Museum does not exaggerate when it describes it as 'the valley of ghosts'. It can feel eerie and haunted with ghostly presences, perhaps nowhere more so than on its wooded western slopes, where the ruins of Poltalloch House, built in Jacobean style between 1849 and 1853 and partially demolished in 1957, protrude spookily through dense trees and shrubs and give every appearance of being one of Ratcliffe Barnett's 'castles of the dead'. Yet at the same time, the valley is refreshingly open and exudes a sense of order. Death here has not been hidden away, and certainly not tamed or minimised. Rather it has been recognised, acknowledged and integrated into the landscape through rituals and memorials in a way that is both calming and reassuring, an effect enhanced by the River Add flowing sluggishly through the valley in giant serpent-like loops. It is the perfect place in which to begin an exploration of the Highland approach to death.

There is undoubtedly a primeval quality to the valley and especially to the Mòine Mhór, or 'Great Moss', one of the last remaining raised peat bogs in Britain, stretching from the gravel terrace on which the village of Kilmartin is sited down to Loch Crinan, where it turns into a salt marsh. It was formed, as was the valley as a whole, by melting ice and rising sea levels at the end of the last Ice Age 10,000 years ago. Although the Mòine Mhór was drained 200 years ago for farming, its designation as a National Nature Reserve since 1987 has allowed water levels to rise and its distinctive springy sphagnum moss to flourish. An important contributor to the battle against global warming, it absorbs huge amounts of carbon dioxide, which is stored in the peat. This is in no sense a desolate landscape – it does not have the barren bleakness of the much more boggy land that covers so much of the northern Highlands and the Outer Hebrides, and it teems with wildlife and especially with wild flowers. It does, however, have an undeniably otherworldly quality. In part, this comes from the mist that so often rises and gathers over it. It is not difficult to imagine dinosaurs lumbering out of the gloom.

Watery sites like mosses, bogs, rivers and lakes have always been places of veneration and seen as the dwelling places of spirits and divinities. As we shall see, they have been favoured places for burials. In the case of the Mòine Mhór, it is more than just its dampness which creates a somewhat mysterious and liminal atmosphere. The moss can feel safe and reassuring, especially at its southern boundary, where the neat houses and beautifully maintained locks along the Crinan Canal create a toytown landscape. But it also provides a bridge to the next world. This is especially true at Crinan itself, where the canal opens out into the sea, letting boats sail to the islands of the west.

We do not know how far those who created that first coffin road in the Kilmartin Valley shared the widespread ancient belief that the ultimate resting place of the dead was to be found far out in the west in the islands beyond the setting sun. This was certainly the view of the Ancient Egyptians whose conception of the afterlife, or *Duat*, centred on the idea that the land of the dead lay beyond the western horizon where the sun went when it died. This, too, was where the Ancient Greeks located the islands of the blessed which they described as Elysium, and it was where the Celts sought the promised land beyond the setting sun far out in the western sea, which they called Tír na nÓg.

Maybe a similar sense of where the next world was located was in the minds of those who first carried the cremated remains of their loved ones for burial in the Kilmartin Valley. It is certainly a thought that has come to much more recent visitors to this first coffin road – especially those visiting its southern end, where the Mòine Mhór gives way to Loch Crinan and the open sea. So it was for that inveterate pilgrim to the West Highlands, Thomas Ratcliffe Barnett, as he stood on a summer's day in 1933 at Crinan harbour looking out from the great flats of the Mòine Mhór 'steeped in the shimmering light of the west' to the islands in the Sound of Jura and beyond to the western ocean: 'You may think you have come to a cul-de-sac of the world. But, before long, you will be quite sure that where the world ends heaven only begins . . . When the sun goes down in all its glory, the outgait to the west from Loch Crinan is like the forecourt of heaven.'[9]

2

Towards the Shrine of a Saint
The Street of the Dead, Iona

The Street of the Dead (Straid nam Marbh) on Iona, which runs
from Martyrs' Bay (Port nam Mairtear) just south of the island's
main pier and ferry terminal up towards the abbey, was the final
link in a chain of coffin roads across the Scottish mainland on
which the bodies of the great and the good were taken for burial
close to the remains of St Columba, who died on the island
in 597.

The best-attested route went through Glen Orchy to the north
shore of Loch Awe, from where coffins were taken by boat to
Kames Bay and then unloaded to continue their overland journey
though the String of Lorn to the aptly named Carraig nam
Marbh, the Rock of the Dead, near Kilninver on the south side of
Loch Feochan, where they began a sea journey, either directly to
Iona or to Port nam Marbh on the north side of the entrance to
Loch Spelve on Mull. From there a well-established coffin road,
which later became a drovers' road, went through Glen More and
down the north side of the Ross of Mull, following the line now
taken by the single track road to Fionnphort.[1] Whichever way
they came, the coffins made their final seaborne journey across
the Sound of Mull, being landed on the east coast of Iona at Port
nam Mairtear – which is perhaps more accurately translated as

the Port of the Dead rather than Martyrs' Bay, as it is usually referred to today.

There is another, earlier, roadway on Iona which takes a very similar course to the coffin road. A section of it, in the form of a two-metre-wide track cobbled with large, water-rounded, tightly packed red granite boulders from the Ross of Mull, is clearly evident running from the wall enclosing the main graveyard on Iona, the Reilig Odhráin, to St Martin's Cross in front of the main west entrance to the abbey. It was part of a carefully laid out processional route for pilgrims coming to venerate St Columba's shrine, designed to make them think of their own mortality and turn their thoughts towards death. Although the term *Straid nam Marbh*, or 'Street of the Dead', should strictly speaking only be used for the later coffin road which was surfaced with a gravel spread, the name has come to be applied to this cobbled roadway, which was revealed in excavations by the Cornish archaeologist Charles Thomas between 1956 and 1963. Thomas himself identi- fied this roadway as the Street of the Dead, and the two Scottish archaeologists who have interpreted his findings, Ewan Campbell and Adrián Maldonado from Glasgow University, feel that it is reasonable to use that term to describe it.[2]

So there are really two streets of the dead on Iona, one a proces- sional way leading to St Columba's shrine and the other a coffin road to bring the bodies of those who wished to be buried near to it. Both have played a key part in establishing the landscape of death that centred on the presence on the island of the corporeal remains of its most famous inhabitant.

Death and what followed it loomed large in the thinking of Columba and his Celtic Christian contemporaries. They were preoccupied with the notion of judgement and the prospect of an eternity spent in either heaven or hell, both of which were conceived of in literal terms. 'Altus Prosator', a rather forbidding

Latin poem which is the most likely of the many works attributed to Columba to come from his own hand, dwells much on the second coming of Christ and the general resurrection which will be heralded by the sounding of the Archangel's trumpet. Tombs will break open, the dead will rise out of their graves, 'their bones gathering to the joints' and 'their ethereal souls meeting them', and 'we shall stand trembling before the Lord's judgement seat'. The poem goes on to describe both hell and heaven in graphic terms, the former filled with darkness, sulphurous fires, worms and other 'dreadful animals' and constant screaming, wailing and gnashing of teeth, the latter with its fountains and rivers, trees bearing a never-ending crop of fruit and 'indescribable and abundant delights'. Although some will undoubtedly be cast into the fiery furnaces, the faithful, and those who have despised the world, will fly off into the heavens to meet Christ, attended by thousands of angels singing hymns and 'rejoicing in holy dances'.[3]

Hell receives rather more attention than heaven in the 'Altus Prosator', reflecting the widespread fear of damnation and its consequences in the early Middle Ages. However, there are also many early Irish texts from monasteries like Iona that dwell on the joys of heaven. Closely modelled on descriptions in the Book of Revelation, they enthuse about the celestial city with its streets paved with gold, angelic choirs and trees bearing luscious fruit and filled with birds singing in their branches.

While it was believed that some saints and martyrs made a direct ascent to heaven, for most mortals there was thought to be a long intermediate state following death and before eventual judgement and resurrection. Although this was often conceived of in terms of sleep, the soul in this intermediate state was not completely immune from what was happening either on earth or in heaven. The prayers of the living as well as the intercessions of the saints could exercise a strong and beneficent influence on the dead. The monastic Rule of Colmcille, probably not drawn up by Columba (Colmcille) himself but by his successors as abbots of the family of monasteries that he founded, enjoined fervent prayer for the dead 'as if every dead person were a particular friend of yours' and the singing of hymns for departed souls.

Columba is portrayed by his biographer, Adomnán, the ninth abbot of Iona, as possessing the gift of prophecy and especially of being able to predict when people were going to die. Indeed, he is often taken to be the first Gael endowed with the power of second sight. On one occasion he is described as sending two monks to tell Cailtan, the abbot of a small monastic community on Loch Awe, to come to see him immediately. Cailtan obeyed the summons and when he arrived on Iona Columba told him, 'I sent for you to come here because I love you as a friend and want you to be able to end your life with me here in true obedience. For before the end of the week you will go in peace to the Lord'. Adomnán goes on to report that before the week was out, Cailtan had, indeed, died.

This is just one example of how thin the boundary was between the worlds of the living and the dead. The dead could help the living, just as they could also be assisted by the prayers of those still on earth. The doctrine of the communion of saints and the image of the great cloud of heavenly witnesses described in the Epistle to the Hebrews as encompassing Christians on earth were both prominent in Celtic Christianity. This meant that death was to be welcomed and embraced as well as dreaded. It was certainly to be carefully prepared for as part of the great journey and pilgrimage of faith in which the believer was always accompanied by God. In the opening words of another poem attributed to Columba, 'Alone with none but Thee, my God, I journey on my way. What need I fear when thou art near, oh king of night and day?'

Columba's own death, which took place on 9 June 597 as he knelt before the altar during the midnight service in the small wooden chapel of the monastery that he had founded on Iona, is movingly described by Adomnán, writing around a hundred years after it occurred:

> The saint, as we have been told by some who were present, even before his soul departed, opened wide his eyes and looked round him from side to side, with a countenance full of wonderful joy and gladness, no doubt seeing the holy angels coming to meet him. Diarmit [Columba's servant] then raised the holy right hand of the saint, that he might bless his assembled monks. And the venerable father himself moved his hand at the same time, as well as he was able, that, as he could not in words while his soul was departing, he might at least, by the motion of his hand, be seen to bless his brethren. And having given them his holy benediction in this way, he immediately breathed his last. After his soul had left the tabernacle of the body, his face still continued ruddy, and brightened in a wonderful way by his vision of the angels, and that to such a degree that he had the appearance not so much of one dead, as of one alive and sleeping.

> I must not omit to mention the revelation made to a certain saint of Ireland, at the very time the blessed soul departed. A holy man named Lugud, one who had grown old in the service of Christ, and was noted for his sanctity and wisdom, had a vision which at early dawn he told to one called Fergnous, who was like himself a servant of Christ. 'In the middle of this last night,' said he, 'Columba, the pillar of many churches, passed to the Lord; and at the moment of his blessed departure, I saw

in the spirit the whole island of Iona, where I never was
in the body, resplendent with the brightness of angels;
and the whole heavens above it, up to the very zenith,
were illumined with the brilliant light of the same heavenly messengers, who descended in countless numbers
to bear away his holy soul. At the same moment, also,
I heard the loud hymns and entrancingly sweet canti-
cles of the angelic host, as his holy soul was borne aloft
amidst the ascending choirs of angels.'[4]

This moving description introduces several themes that were
to remain prominent in the Hebridean and Highland approach
to death and dying for well over a thousand years. Perhaps
most striking is the presence of angels, seen by the dying as visible beings coming down from heaven to meet them and also
apparent to others as heavenly messengers bearing away the souls
of those who have died and singing as they do so. There is also
the mystical awareness of a death happening in a faraway place,
again indicative of second sight, and the ambiguity between the
orthodox Christian doctrine of the post-mortem state as a long
period of sleep before a general resurrection and the popular belief
in the immortality of the soul and a more immediate passage to
heaven after death.

Following Columba's death, there were three days and nights
of mourning, with prayers and chants. His burial was a simple
and austere service attended only by his fellow monks. There was
no coffin or elaborate tombstone. His body was wrapped in a
linen shroud and the stone that he had used as a pillow was set
beside his shallow grave to mark it. This reflected the humility
that he had shown throughout his life and the Christian belief,
contrary to the thinking behind the laying out of the Kilmartin
Valley, that the departed soul was safely in the hands of God and

needed no great memorial nor any material aids to ease the passage into the next world.

Columba was not allowed to rest in his simple underground
grave for long. In the 150 years after his death a cult grew up
around him, thanks in large part to the Life written by Adomnán
and other hagiographical eulogies which promoted his sanctity
and portrayed him as a miracle worker, prophet and visionary.
Around the middle of the eighth century his remains were rein-
terred, together with his sacred bell, books, staff and tunic, in an
elaborate elevated casket shrine on the site of the chapel which
now stands to the left of the great west door of Iona Abbey. This
re-enshrinement was almost certainly partially inspired by the
broader cult of saints which swept over Christian Europe in this
period, producing a heightened sense of their miraculous powers
and continued spiritual presence, exerted through their corporeal
relics and greatly stimulating pilgrimage to their shrines. It was
around the same time that the legend emerged of the coming
of St Andrew's bones to a Pictish settlement in north-east Fife,
which would lead to the building of Scotland's largest cathedral,
at St Andrews, and the development of a cult which culminated
in the apostle trumping the Gael as patron saint of Scotland.

It was after the enshrinement of Columba's relics that the
processional route was developed to take the growing number of
pilgrims coming to Iona from their landing place near the present
ferry terminal on Iona up the gentle hill to the saint's shrine.
More of the cobbled roadway was revealed after Charles Thomas's
initial excavation at Iona Abbey during clearance work in 1963.
Building it must have been a massive operation – it has been
estimated that the section within the monastic enclosure alone
would have required the procurement and transport of well over
250 tons of stone from Mull. The later coffin road, built to carry
bodies for burial near to the saint's remains, was excavated in 2013

and found to have a different character, being surfaced with a gravel spread.

The building of the cobbled processional way, which is what visitors to Iona see today as they make their way to the abbey, reflected a renewed interest in dramatising and revivifying the faith by encouraging people to walk symbolically in the footsteps of Christ on the way to his crucifixion at Calvary. It created a ritual landscape deliberately created to induce thoughts of mortality and the journey to salvation in the minds of those who walked it.

It was almost certainly consciously modelled on the route to the Church of the Holy Sepulchre in Jerusalem known as the Via Dolorosa. Significantly, it was constructed at the same time that many churches were establishing Stations of the Cross in their buildings so that those who could not physically go to Jerusalem could walk symbolically in Jesus' footsteps. This new emphasis on walking the faith chimed in with a renewed interest in sacred space and holy places aroused by works such as Adomnán's *De Locis Sanctis*, written on Iona at the end of the seventh century, which dwelt much on both the earthly and the heavenly Jerusalem. The processional roadway on Iona, which has come to be known as the Street of the Dead, was laid out to link these two places, with Columba's shrine representing both Christ's tomb in the earthly Jerusalem and also the dwelling place of the saints in the heavenly city. It took pilgrims to the holiest place on the island and gave them a foretaste of heaven.

The roadway was flanked by at least seven high-standing crosses erected during the later eighth and early ninth centuries along the processional pilgrim route to Columba's shrine. Only one of them, St Martin's Cross, remains in its entirety and in its original location today, standing as an iconic feature of Iona's spiritual landscape and being the gathering point for the weekly pilgrimage around the island organised by the Iona Community. Carved from a single block of grey epidorite (granite) rock, probably from the Argyll mainland, it stands 16 feet 8 inches high in its stepped box. Fragments of three other crosses, dedicated respectively to St Matthew, St John and St Oran, have been sensitively reassembled and are now displayed in the museum behind the abbey, and a concrete replica of St John's Cross stands in front of the chapel built on the presumed site of Columba's shrine next to the west door of the restored Benedictine abbey. The dramatic scenes from well-known biblical stories, many of them involving deliverance from danger, carved on the faces of these crosses, were clearly designed to enhance the spiritual atmosphere and graphically illustrate cardinal points of the Christian faith.

Together, the high-standing crosses that originally stood along the processional pilgrim route on Iona form the finest collection in the British Isles of these distinctive and elaborate expressions of early medieval Christianity, representing the culmination of the sculptor's art first displayed in the chiselling out of a simple cross design on a block of stone. They are in a real sense the direct successors of the enigmatic standing stones in the Kilmartin Valley and the crude incised gravestones in early Christian cemeteries like Cladh a' Bhile in mid-Argyll. We have already noted the tradition from prehistoric times in the Highlands and Islands of using stones as markers of burials. In early Christian understanding, they were seen as protecting the dead and ensuring their salvation by literally making the sign of the cross over their bodies through a crude and simple carving on the surface of the stones.

On Iona, crosses marked the place of death as well as the place of burial. Adomnán noted that a cross was erected in front of the door to the monastery's grain kiln where Columba's uncle, Earnan, had died while he was visiting Iona, and another at the spot where Columba himself was standing at the moment of his uncle's death. These were probably made of wood rather than stone, although Adomnán reported that they were still standing well over a hundred years after they had been erected. But when it came to marking burials, it was stone that was generally used. The earliest example of a West Highland cross-marked stone that can be dated with any accuracy was found on Iona and is now displayed near the entrance to the museum behind the abbey. It is unusual in that it has lettering on its top edge. The Latin inscription *Lapis Echodi* has been taken to indicate that it marked the grave of Eochaid Buide, King of Dál Riata, who died in 629. It is significant, but no surprise, that this earliest dateable cross-incised stone, almost certainly carved and erected within a generation of Columba's death, marked a grave.

The medieval cult of the saints stimulated among the Christian faithful not just the wish to make pilgrimages to saints' shrines in a quest to connect with their power through touching their relics, but also a more radical desire to die and to be buried near them. The attraction of dying, or at least being buried, close to Columba on Iona was reinforced by the feeling that one should go west towards the setting sun to die and by the continuing strong belief that the promised land of eternal life lay among the islands of the blessed in the western sea. Many would have echoed the sentiments of a statement attributed to Adomnán and now stencilled on the wall in the entrance to the cloisters of Iona Abbey: 'If I be destined to die in Iona, it were a merciful leave taking. I know not under the blue sky a better spot for death.' Even if you did not manage to die there, you could contrive to be buried there, if you had the money, the power and the influence. Being laid to rest near Columba brought you closer to God and further on the journey to heaven. In that way, Iona became important and attractive as a gateway to the afterlife. Contemporary Irish annals record several Irish kings and princes journeying 'in pilgrimage and penance' to spend their last years on the island in the late eighth century. They include Niall Frossach, King of Tara, who died there in 788, and Artgal, King of Connacht, who died in 791.

It was to cater for this demand for burials on the island that the cemetery at the Reilig Odhráin (the burial place of Odhráin) was created, and the coffin road that more properly warrants the title of Street of the Dead was constructed from the Port of the Dead where bodies were unloaded after their long journeys across land and sea. The Reilig Odhráin was sited outside the monastic ditch or *vallum* – the monks had their own graveyard within the precincts – and seems to have been created as a burial ground for lay people, including visitors, penitents who came to the monastery seeking what would now be called pastoral counselling, and local people. It came to be the place where wealthy and powerful clan chiefs, kings and princes also sought burial.

Guidebooks suggest that numerous early kings of Scotland were buried on Iona, a notion propagated by the fact that the Street of the Dead is sometimes also referred to as 'The Road of the Kings'. There is, in fact, some doubt as to just how many royal graves there are. Accounts of Scottish and Norwegian kings being buried on Iona first surfaced in the fourteenth century. When Donald Monro, Archdeacon of the Isles, visited the island in 1549, he was told that four Irish, eight Scandinavian and 48 Scottish kings, including Macbeth, were buried in the Reilig Odhráin. He was shown three chapels, each with a marble slab, engraved respectively in Latin 'Grave of the Kings of Scotland', 'Grave of the Kings of Ireland' and 'Grave of the Kings of Norway'. The antiquarian and travel writer Martin Martin, visiting the island around 1695, was given similar information but noted that the individual inscriptions on the royal tombs had worn off and there were only later generic inscriptions, presumably those seen by

Monro. By the time James Boswell got there in 1773 with Samuel
Johnson he was disappointed to find 'only some grave-stones flat
on the earth and we could see no inscriptions. How far short
was this of marble monuments, like those in Westminster Abbey,
which I had imagined here.' Dr Johnson took a somewhat sceptical view, noting that: 'Iona has long enjoyed, without any very
credible attestation, the honour of being reputed the cemetery of
Scottish kings. It is not unlikely that, when the opinion of local
sanctity was prevalent, the chieftains of the isles, and perhaps
some of the Norwegian or Irish princes, were reposited in this
venerable enclosure. But by whom the subterranean vaults are
peopled is now utterly unknown.'[5]

There is, in fact, no actual evidence that the kings of Dál Riata
from the sixth to the ninth century were buried on the island, and
Dr James Fraser of Edinburgh University has persuasively argued
that the notion of Iona as the mausoleum of early Scottish kings
was a fiction invented by King Alexander I in the early twelfth
century. Wanting to present his immediate antecedents, Margaret
and Malcolm, as representatives of a new dynasty buried in
Dunfermline, Alexander consigned earlier Scottish monarchs to
Iona to suggest that they belonged firmly to the past.[6] Despite this
scepticism, however, Ewan Campbell and Adrián Maldonado,
the most recent archaeologists to turn their attention to Iona,
are quite certain that several early medieval kings (among them
the already mentioned Eoichaid Buide) were buried there. Several
sources claim that Ecgfrith, King of Northumbria, was buried on
Iona after being killed in the Battle of Nechtansmere in 685, and a
tenth-century poem about the burial of Bruide mac Bile, King of
the Picts, who died in 692, in 'an old hollow oak trunk' may tie in
with evidence of early log burials found beside Columba's shrine
chapel. The Norse king of Dublin, Olaf Sihtricsson, is recorded
as having retired to and died on Iona in 980.[7]

Even if we cannot be certain that Scotland's early kings were buried on the island, there is no doubt that the bodies of a good many chieftains and nobles were carried up the Street of the Dead. Iona's appeal as a final resting place can be gauged by the fact that excavations have revealed at least seven burial grounds on the tiny and sparsely populated island. The graves within them show the influence of Christianity and are very different from the cists and henges in Kilmartin Valley. Whole corpses were interred, rather than just cremated remains, the bodies orientated east–west, and there are no mounds, chambers or grave goods, just simple graves dug in the earth, some but not all marked by a stone.

The most impressive and important of these burial grounds was undoubtedly the Reilig Odhráin. It takes its name from a contemporary of Columba's, often now shortened and anglicised to St Oran, about whose own death several somewhat bizarre legends developed. One version that seems to date from the twelfth century has it that he was buried alive as a voluntary human sacrifice because Columba was told that the walls of a chapel that he was trying to build would not stand until a living man was buried below the foundations. Some days after his burial, Oran apparently popped out of the ground to announce that 'there is no Hell as you suppose, nor Heaven that people talk about'. Columba hastily had his body removed and reburied in consecrated ground. In another, later, version of the story, Oran was buried with the promise that his soul would be safe in heaven. Sometime after his burial, Columba had him exhumed and Oran, who was still alive, tried to climb out of his grave but Columba had it quickly filled in to save his soul from the world and its sin.

A third version of the story, recorded by Alexander Carmichael in the late nineteenth century in places 'widely apart' including the Outer Hebrides, Lochaber and Tiree, has Oran deliberately burying himself alive to test the Church's view of the afterlife after debating the subject with Columba. When his grave was opened three days later, he opened his eyes and said:

> Nor is heaven as is alleged,
> Nor is hell as is asserted,
> Nor are the good eternally happy,
> Nor are the bad eternally unhappy.

This prompted Columba's response:

> Earth, earth upon the eye of Oran,
> Before he wakes more controversy
> Lest scandal should be given to the faith,
> Lest offence should be given to the brethren.

Earth was promptly piled up over Oran and he was buried permanently.[8]

It is difficult to know what to make of these stories, which could be taken to suggest that life goes on after death much as it has on earth and that there is neither heaven nor hell in the sense that they have been normally understood in Christian tradition. Roger McLean, an Anglican priest who studied Gaelic folklore, wrote in the preface to his *Poems of the Western Highlanders*, in which the verses collected by Carmichael about Oran appear: 'the story of St Oran was swiftly utilised to symbolise the reality and the certainty of the afterlife, doubts and questions being met by the vivid but unsatisfactory tale'.[9] I wonder if in fact it rather represented a popular reaction to the focus on a literal hell and heaven in the teaching of the Church and signalled that there was much scepticism about this doctrine.

The rather bizarre story of Oran and his post-mortem experiences has not stopped people wanting to be buried in the Reilig

Odhráin in relatively recent times. Those interred there include Marjory Kennedy-Fraser, the singer, collector of Hebridean folk-songs, pioneer feminist and pacifist who died in 1930, and John Smith, the leader of the British Labour Party from 1992 until his death in 1994, whose grave carries an epitaph drawn from the fourth epistle of *An Essay on Man*, by Alexander Pope: 'An honest man's the noblest work of God.' Both made their final journeys along the Street of the Dead.

Visitors to Iona today often feel a closeness to the dead. In the famous (borrowed) words of George MacLeod, the Church of Scotland minister who rebuilt the monastic buildings around the Benedictine abbey and founded the Iona Community in the 1930s, it is a 'thin place', where this world and the next seem close. Columba's presence still pervades the island, even if his remains were long ago removed to Kells in Ireland and Dunkeld in Perthshire to prevent their being seized by marauding Vikings. The Hill of the Angels, where the saint is said to have communed with angels as he stood with his arms upraised in prayer, is a prominent landmark halfway down the road that bisects the island and leads down to the machair on its western side. Those walking up towards the abbey from the ferry jetty near the Port of the Dead are close to if not actually on the route of the coffin road that brought so many to their final resting place. If they pause in front of St Mark's Cross they will have stepped onto the processional way that was created to remind pilgrims of their mortality and their journey to salvation in the heavenly Jerusalem. It is impossible to go far on Iona without setting foot on one of its streets of the dead.

3

Intimations of Heaven
Jura

Another island in the west, Jura, like Iona, was a favoured place in which to die and be buried. As well as having coffin roads to its own three graveyards, Jura also seems to have served as a staging post on coffin routes from south Argyll to Iona and Oronsay, where the precincts of the priory dedicated to Columba became another popular burial place for those who could afford the long journey there. An intriguing entry in the 1845 *Statistical Account of Argyll* by the minister of Jura from 1823 to 1849, Alexander Kennedy, who was my great-great-great grandfather, mentions the many caves on the uninhabited west side of the island: 'Two of them are called corpachs, i.e. places where the inhabitants of Jura and other countries, on their way to Oransay and Iona to bury their dead, were in the habit of depositing the corpses of their friends, until a favourable opportunity of prosecuting their voyage to Iona and Oransay occurred. One of these corpachs is in Rhuintalen, opposite to Colonsay: the other, called the corpach of I Columkill, is several miles to the north-east, along the coast.'[1]

The current Ordnance Survey map shows both Corpach Bay and Cnoc na Corpaich just north of the raised beaches on the west coast of Jura, opposite Colonsay, suggesting that this is where bodies must have been rested and then embarked for their final journey to Oronsay or Iona. The Gaelic word *corpach* means 'place of the dead'. The village with that name four miles north of Fort William on the north shore of Loch Linnhe is thought to be so called because it, too, was a resting place on a more northerly coffin road to Iona.

There are other place names on Jura that could also refer to stopping places on old coffin roads. One such is Geata Àth nam Marbh (the gate of the ford of the dead), about a mile north of Jura House by the side of the one and only road up the island. This could have been where coffins were rested when being brought up from Ardfin on the south of the island to the cemetery at Keils above Craighouse. In island legend and tradition it is regarded, as its name implies, as providing a passage between this world and the next. Other legends locate both the underworld and the home of the ocean gods in the turbulent waters beneath the famous Corryvreckan whirlpool off the island's north coast. Jura is, indeed, a good place in which to explore the Celtic understanding of the otherworld, with its location among the islands in the western ocean, and to assess how far this belief continued after the coming of Christianity.

There is much debate among Celtic scholars about whether the *immrama*, the Old Irish tales recounting heroic sea journeys to the otherworld, are primarily pagan or Christian in their influence and message. Some treat the pagan otherworld as almost indistinguishable from the Christian afterlife, but others have been keen to make a clear distinction between them. In her book *Otherworlds: Fantasy and History in Mediaeval Literature*, Aisling Byrne initially sounds a note of caution, insisting that the otherworld 'cannot easily be subsumed into the idea of the afterlife, Christian or otherwise'. Yet she goes on to say: 'The distinction between secular and religious otherworlds is not as absolute as it might at first appear. Descriptions of religious otherworlds frequently utilise imagery that echoes that of more secular realms. This partly results from the fact that both are, to some extent, drawing on the same pool of biblical and apocryphal imagery.'[2]

One of the most famous of the early medieval Celtic *immrama* is the *Immram Brain* (Voyage of Bran), which probably dates from the late seventh or early eighth century. It tells of Bran mac Febail, an Irish prince who embarks on a quest for the other-world, inspired by the visit of a lady 'in strange raiment' who appears in his palace bearing a silver branch from Emain Ablach (the land of apples), a mythical island across the western waves which she describes to him in song:

> There is an island far away,
> Around which seahorses glisten;
> Pillars of white bronze are under it,
> Shining through aeons of beauty.
>
> Unknown is wailing or treachery
> In the familiar cultivated land,
> There is nothing rough or harsh,
> But sweet music striking on the ear.
>
> Without sorrow, without grief, without death,
> Without any sickness, without weakness,
> But sweet music striking on the ear,
> That is the character of Emain.[3]

There is considerable similarity between this description and the accounts of Paradise in early Irish Christian literature. *Fis Adamnán* (The Vision of Adomnán), which purports to be a vision of the next world experienced by Columba's biographer and has been dated as early as the eighth century, although the earliest manuscript source is 300 years after this, portrays heaven in similar terms, with a particular emphasis on the sweet music provided by angels and birds singing in the trees.

In his book *Poacher's Pilgrimage*, which recounts his own twelve-day walk through the adjoined Hebridean islands of Lewis and Harris, Alastair McIntosh reflects on the *immrama* and quotes the view of the leading Celticist John Carey that they achieved an 'imaginative reconciliation' between paganism and Christianity and reflect 'the perfection of human nature as God had first intended it'. For McIntosh himself, the realms across the water in Celtic mythology (Tír na nÓg, etc.), 'belong to the ever-young, a cosmic homecoming, the end of all our *nostos-algos*. Here life's full bloom, its fullness of potential, its beauty is reconstituted.'[4]

The best-known example of a clearly Christian *immram* is the Voyage of St Brendan (*Navigatio Sancti Brendani*), which describes the journey of the sixth-century Irish monk Brendan of Clonfert and his companions across the Atlantic in search of the island of the blessed (also called the Land of Promise of the Saints, or *Terra Repromissionis Sanctorum*). First recounted in a manuscript dating from the early tenth century, it became easily the most popular of all the *immrama* and has been described as 'a medieval best seller'.[5] The story has been interpreted in several ways, including as an allegory of the monastic life, but it seems most likely that it was designed to illustrate the journey from this world to the next.

When, after many adventures, Brendan and his companions eventually reach the island of the blessed, they find it to be very like both the *Emain Ablach* described in the Voyage of Bran and the new heaven and new earth described in the Book of Revelation. All its stones are precious gems, every tree bears fruit, there is no sadness or sorrow and no sense of ageing or decay. The voyagers meet a 'young man of resplendent features, and very handsome aspect' who tells them: 'This is the land you have sought after for so long a time; but you could not hitherto find it, because Christ our Lord wished first to display to you His divers mysteries in this immense ocean. Return now to the land of your birth, bearing with you as much of those fruits and of those precious stones, as your boat can carry; for the days of your earthly pilgrimage must draw to a close, when you may rest in peace among your saintly brethren. After many years this land will be made manifest to those who come after you.'[6]

Is it the Garden of Eden that is being described here, or is it heaven? Are they, indeed, one and the same place? Certainly, this is how the next world was conceived in Celtic literature and it is not surprising that islands like Jura came to be identified as having the characteristics of Tír na nÓg. It is in this context that Geata Àth nam Marbh was seen as providing a passageway from this world to the next. It was not the only such place in the Hebrides and the Highlands. Some were associated with hell rather than heaven, like Clach-Tholl, a raised natural arch located south-west of Port Appin at the end of the Appin peninsula which was seen as a tunnel leading to hell. But the majority, especially in the Hebridean islands, were seen as gateways and pointers to heaven, confirming that they were, indeed, the promised isles of the blessed.

It is not difficult to feel intimations of heaven on Jura, especially perhaps when standing in one of the three main island graveyards, which are among the most evocative and atmospheric in Scotland. The oldest and largest, Kilearnadil, sits in the hills beyond the crofting township of Kiels and some distance above Craighouse, the main settlement, with spectacular views east out over the Sound of Jura to Knapdale and the Kintyre peninsula and to the mountains of Arran beyond. The graveyard at Tarbert, halfway up the island, stands in a field close to the sea and is guarded by a ruined chapel which has an early dedication to Columba. The smallest and most northerly graveyard on Jura, at Kilchianaig near Inverlussa, is a secluded and quiet haven screened by trees with the River Lussa flowing peacefully alongside it. There are at least another five burial places on the island, including a group of graves marked by a broken stone beside the road to Inver on the south-west coast. They are said to be where a number of sailors were buried after they had died of fever when their ship was anchored in Whitefarland Bay in the Sound of Islay. A patch of ground above the shoreline of the Corran sands at Loch na Mile a little north of Craignish supposedly contains the bodies of a number of MacDonalds killed in battle and of 13 stillborn children, all members of the same family, on whom a curse had been placed.

Kilearnadil graveyard, which like Kilchianaig is still in use and provides a continuing link with the long and distinctive tradition of Highland and Hebridean funerals, is on the site of what is thought to have been the first ecclesiastical settlement on Jura, which gave its name to the parish covering the south of the island. A church stood there throughout the Middle Ages, dedicated to Earnan (possibly the uncle of Columba), who was supposedly the first abbot of a monastery which his nephew had established on Jura. According to local tradition, Earnan died while on a visit to Iona. In accordance with his wishes, his body was taken back to Jura, landed on a rock subsequently known as Leac Earnan, and buried in the first glen where a cloud of mist appeared. As the first person to be buried there, he gave his name to the graveyard. An alternative foundation legend for Kilearnadil suggests that Earnan was buried in the precincts of his monastery where there may already have been monks' graves.

The graveyard is now accessed via steps leading up to a relatively recent southern extension. There is another, more modern,

extension to the north. The central and oldest part of the graveyard contains several recumbent table tombs, including one to my
great-great-great grandfather, Rev. Alexander Kennedy, although
the inscription is now indecipherable. It is dominated by the
imposing mausoleum, built in 1838 by the architect William Burn
to house the grave slabs and monuments to the Campbell lairds
of Jura dating back to the early seventeenth century. This is now
in a somewhat unsafe state and surrounded by a protective fence
as well as its original iron railings. Below the mausoleum, along
the eastern side of the cemetery, runs a fast-flowing stream which
has its source high up among the Paps of Jura and continues its
course towards the sea past the former manse, giving rise to its
name of *Abhuinn a Mhinisteir*, or the Minister's Burn. In the
words of Peter Youngson, a former minister of the island, 'its
chuckle breaks the stillness of the place where the majority of Jura
funerals still take place with absence of haste and quiet dignity'.[7]
Highland and Island graveyards were almost invariably sited next
to a stream, supposedly to allow the swift passage of departed
souls down to the sea, perhaps on their journey to the isles of
the blessed or maybe to God's ocean depths in which the blind
Church of Scotland minister, George Matheson, felt that the flow
of our lives would be richer and fuller when we eventually gave
them back to God (see p. 114).

What probably most intrigues visitors who make their way up
to the cemetery today is the plaque near the entrance in the south-
west corner commemorating Gillouir MacCrain who, according
to Martin Martin, 'kept one hundred and eighty Christmasses
in his own house' before he died around 1645. Martin obtained
this unlikely story from several of MacCrain's surviving friends
and acquaintances, all of whom vouched for its accuracy, during
his 1695 tour of the Western Isles. Modern guidebooks tend to
offer the explanation that changes to the calendar made in the

seventeenth century allowed for Christmas to be celebrated on two different dates and that perhaps Gillouir MacCrain was actually 90 when he died. Whatever the truth, he is not the only one of his family to be credited with a remarkably long life. Among the graves in Kilchianaig cemetery near Inverlussa is one to his descendant, Mary MacCrain, recording her death in 1856 at the age of 128.

There is a wonderfully evocative description of a burial in one of the Jura graveyards by Charles John Shore, 2nd Baron Teignmouth, an English politician and writer who made two tours of the 'coasts and islands of Scotland' in the late 1820s. Although his early reference to its taking place on a 'distant knoll' would suggest its location as being Kilearnadil with its elevated site, the distance that he later specifies from the graveyard to the Port Askaig ferry and the references to the proximity of Lagg Bay and to Tarbert suggest that it must have been the Tarbert cemetery. It is worth quoting in full.

> On landing and reaching a height, in the midst of the waste howling wilderness, for wind and rain augmented the dreariness of the scene, I perceived on a distant knoll a solitary black spot, which might have been mistaken by an unpractised eye for a sign, infallible to the sportsman, of the place of his wounded quarry, a collection of crows or corbies, employed in accelerating the death or devouring the carcass of the poor animal. It proved, however, on near approach, to be a band of mourners assembled at a rustic funeral, on an ancient and perfectly sequestered cemetery, distinguished by the ruins of a chapel. A grave was digging to receive the remains of a shepherd of the laird of Jura; and beside the coffin lay two others, containing the bodies of his

children, one of whom had been buried two years, and the other one year, and were now taken up to make room for their parent.

When the grave was closed, the mourners, sixty in number, attended by their dogs, which were very numerous, sat down on the ground, now thoroughly soaked with heavy rain, which had been falling for some hours, and the brother-in-law of the deceased invited me to drink a glass of whisky, and eat some oat-cake. About twenty women and girls were present, among whom were the mother and daughter, accompanied by the sons of the deceased. The mother, nearly seventy years of age, sat fixing her eyes earnestly on the grave, in which were buried her husband, and children, and grand-children, and just sipped the whisky which was first offered to her. The women seemed to dispense with this part of the ceremony, but the men and boys drank their three rounds, according to custom; and abundance of oat-cake was distributed. The repast was concluded with a prayer and thanksgiving in Gaelic, delivered by a brother-in-law of the deceased, who stood up in the midst of the circle, all present being uncovered.

A man from Isla, whom I had asked whether prayer was ever offered on these occasions, replied with obvious suspicion as to the motives of the inquiry, and in a low tone of voice, 'Yes, that is beginning: but it is Popish, and there are no Papists here'; at the same time he had no objection to the commencing and concluding with thanksgiving, which had taken place that day.

The mourners had assembled with the promptitude characteristic of their ancient obedience to any summons to a public occasion, for the deceased had breathed his

last only the day before, at five in the morning. Friends
had been instantly despatched in all directions to different parts of Jura and Isla, inviting the mourners to
the grave at three the following afternoon. The corpse
had been brought half the length of the island that
day and the Isla man, with whom I had conversed,
had walked thirty miles since morning, and intended
returning twenty miles more to the ferry of Portaskaig
that evening. They had well earned the refreshment
provided for them. The ceremony was conducted with
perfect order and solemnity: and the mourners returned
to Tarbert, where boats awaited them. The little pub-
lic-house in Lagg bay, where we landed and I took up
my quarters, was well thronged; and my companions
soon exchanged their demure looks for smiling and
merriment: those who had far to return were induced
to stay, and they continued drinking and singing till
past midnight, making an uproar which prevented the
possibility of sleeping.

The mourners found their reception at Tarbert so
pleasant, that they remained next day, and assisted in
restoring a bridge which had been swept away by a
torrent.[8]

Several of the features noted in this account of a burial on
Jura were common to many Hebridean funerals. The practice of
sharing an oatcake and a dram of whisky around the grave is still
found on Jura today, although not with quite the same level of
consumption as at the one attended by Lord Teignmouth, where
he noted that 'the standard ration is three glasses of raw whisky
per person'. I myself partook of an oatcake and a dram with
fellow mourners around a grave which had not yet been filled

in immediately after a burial at Kilearnadil cemetery in 2013. Teignmouth was struck by the absence of religious ceremony at the funeral and the fact that the brief prayer and thanksgiving were delivered by a relative rather than a minister. This was characteristic of most funerals, at least in the Protestant parts of the Highlands and Islands, throughout the nineteenth century, reflecting the fact that they were organised and conducted by family and friends without the professional assistance of clergy or undertakers. Also striking were the short time that elapsed between death and burial, the long journeys undertaken by mourners as well as by those carrying the corpse along the coffin road, and the carousing that took place after the funeral.

The Jura funeral was not the only one that Lord Teignmouth attended and wrote about during his travels. His accounts provide a fascinating picture of the Hebridean and West Highland approach to death and not least of the sometimes excessive revelry involved. This often started very soon after the death itself. As he put it, 'the funeral and festal preparations are inseparably blended in the mind of the Highlanders'.[9] During a stay in Stornoway, he received an invitation to attend the funeral of a wealthy old lady. 'Immediately after her decease,' he noted, 'a cask of Madeira was opened in her house, a wake had been kept up, and the house nightly illuminated according to the custom of the country.'[10]

The tradition of offering lavish hospitality to the many friends and neighbours who came to pay their last respects to the corpse as it rested in the house was not confined to those who were rich. Lord Teignmouth was one of several observers of the practice to express concern at the financial burden it placed on poor people. Plentiful supplies of liquor, snuff and tobacco were provided by the grieving family, and clay pipes were often bought to be handed out to visitors. It was not unknown for the deceased to have a pipe placed between his or her lips so as not to be left out. As well as being washed and clothed, the corpse was also shaved and sometimes sat up in a chair rather than laid out on a table or bed, so as to be more part of the company. The practice of treating the dead as though they were still part of the family is found in several cultures, perhaps in its most extreme form among the Torajan people on Sulawesi Island in Indonesia. There the dead are not buried but sit for months in temporary houses and are sometimes given a seat in the family home, where they gradually decompose.

Those visiting to pay their respects during the continuous two or three day and night wake that followed death in the Highlands and Hebrides sometimes played cards and parlour games like blind man's buff and even danced around the corpse. Elizabeth Grant of Rothiemurchus recorded that following the death of George Ross, the husband of the Rothiemurchus hen-wife in 1812, after 'a bottle of whisky, or maybe more, had failed to cure him', he 'was waked after the old fashion, shaved and partly dressed, and set up in his bed, all the countryside collecting round him. After abundance of refreshment the company set to dancing when, from the jolting of the floor, out tumbled the corpse into the midst of the reel and away scampered the guests screaming and declaring the old man had come to life again.'[11]

The funeral that Lord Teignmouth attended as a guest in Stornoway was unusual in having a minister, who arrived in an open boat from the mainland, as the chief mourner and also for involving the local parish minister, although in accordance with tradition neither took any part in the actual burial and both left the meal provided afterwards in a tent pitched in the graveyard before things became too raucous:

> The funeral was attended by all the principal inhabitants
> of Stornoway. Our party arrived too late at the house

of the deceased to partake of the preliminary refreshments, but we overtook the procession on the road to the ancient cemetery of Stornoway, which is situated on the beach of Broad Bay, about four miles from the town.

In Scotland, the funeral ceremony is celebrated without any religious rite. The minister of the parish attends only when invited, and not officially. He sometimes embraces the solemn opportunity of offering up a prayer among the assembled mourners at the house of the deceased, previous to the departure of the procession, though he may not accompany it. On the present occasion, as soon as we reached the cemetery, the coffin was deposited in the grave with all possible decency, and the whole body of mourners instantly adjourned to a tent pitched in the cemetery, within a few yards of the mausoleum, where we found tables groaning beneath a plentiful repast.

As soon as we were all arranged, a hundred and twenty in number, the minister, who presided as chief-mourner, delivered a grace in the form of a prayer; and the minister of the parish offered up another, accompanied by thanksgiving after dinner. The bottle was then circulated, and many loyal, patriotic, and complimentary toasts, including the Church of England, and the Kirk of Scotland, followed; nor was the memory of the deceased forgotten, while the toasts were as usual accompanied with appropriate speeches. The presence of several ministers, and one acting as chairman, no doubt tended to preserve a certain degree of sobriety in the midst of revelry and merriment, inseparable from such a meeting. But at length the chord was touched, to which the bosoms of the Islanders responded, amidst the flow of wine and whisky, with resistless accordance. 'The chief of the Macivers' was proposed amidst loud applause. The guests became now quite tumultuous, and the Rev. Chairman immediately rose up and left the tent, accompanied by nearly all the party.

The expectation of the gleanings of so plenteous a repast had attracted to the spot a multitude of people of all ages, who thronged around and closed in upon the tent, eager for the signal for rushing in upon the remains of the feast. A man was constantly employed in walking round the tent, armed with a long whip, with which he inflicted perpetual, but almost fruitless, chastisement on intruders. A few of the guests, who had not heeded the example of the chairman, continued long carousing, and one of them was brought to Stornoway on the bier which conveyed the body to the grave.[12]

Teignmouth gave several other instances of disorderly scenes following funerals, such as this one in the cemetery of Assynt, 'narrated to me by a gentleman present':

The habitation of the deceased was distant from the place of interment. The body was borne on men's shoulders during part of the journey, and then conveyed in a boat over the lake. The bearers became so drunk by frequent recourse to the whisky, that at length there was scarcely found a sufficient number of persons sober enough to deposit the coffin in the boat, many of the attendants being drunk when they left the house of the deceased. When they reached the shore, the body was forgotten, and a detachment was sent in quest of it, after a numerous muster had been made in the churchyard, and the cause of the delay which prevented the last act of the ceremony was ascertained. But the collection of a multitude of fiery spirits, heated by intoxicating liquors, was attended by its probable consequences. The sexton happened to cast up, whilst digging the grave, a large thigh-bone, which proved in very deed a bone of contention. For on the northern shore of Loch Assynt, contiguous to each other, stood an old castle and a mansion-house, in which resided formerly two families, Mackenzies and Macdonalds, between whom a violent feud subsisted. And the bone was of such large size that the Mackenzies claimed it as having belonged to one of their race, a man of gigantic stature. This point was disputed by the other party, and a desperate fight ensued.[13]

There were other funerals where the drinking and feuding resulted in loss of life, including one on Islay where a man was killed in a fight in the graveyard. Lord Teignmouth was struck by the somewhat casual and matter-of-fact attitude that seemed to be taken to objects associated with funerals, particularly coffins. He instanced the example of 'some excellent wheaten bread', which was brought in a coffin with the body of an old lady being conveyed from Inverness to a country graveyard, and later served at the post-burial entertainment. He was also told of a minister on Gigha who 'availed himself of the coffin destined for his wife, which he had made at Campbeltown, as a packing case for groceries and other stores'. This led Teignmouth to ponder what he saw as a strange contradiction at the heart of the Highland approach to death.

Whence arises, it may be asked, revelry so utterly at variance with the feelings of awe or sorrow naturally excited

by death and its solemn accompaniments? It cannot be
attributed to the levity of the people, because none are
accustomed to regard death with more habitual serious-
ness than the natives of these regions. The thought or
mention of his inevitable doom is not discarded by the
Scottish Highlander with affected contempt or incon-
siderate levity, but entertained with becoming solemnity.
Nor does funeral revelry proceed from deficiency of
relative attachment, because the Highlanders are strongly
actuated by this principle; and the very anxiety to provide
for an entertainment suitable to the rank or family of
the deceased results from its operation. Nay, it is often
indulged at the expense of personal feeling, as well as considerable cost, for the relative merges his own grief in the
desire of bestowing appropriate honour on the deceased.[14]

While speculating that the undue and unseemly revelry that
so often accompanied Highland funerals might come from an
over-literal interpretation of the biblical injunction in Proverbs
31.6: 'Give wine unto those that have grief of heart', Teignmouth
felt it had two overriding causes. The first was 'the inebriating
quality of the beverage resorted to on these occasions' and the
other was 'the want of an adequate preventive, a burial-service,
such as is used by some of the Reformed Churches on the con-
tinent, or more especially like that of the Church of England,
repelling mirth and levity by the awful and affecting solemnity
with which it "commits the body to the ground, earth to earth,
ashes to ashes, dust to dust", whilst it represses immoderate grief,
by lifting the dejected spirit of the mourner to "the sure and certain hope of the resurrection of the life to come".'[15]

The lack of prayers and of any formal liturgy at burials in
Scotland was a consequence of profound Presbyterian unease

about anything that smacked of praying for the dead. The First Book of Discipline of 1560 had specifically proscribed any singing or reading at burials on the grounds that it would encourage the superstition that such activities by the living 'may profit the dead'. It instructed that no kind of religious ceremony should accompany burials 'other than that the dead be committed to the grave with such gravity and sobriety as those present may seem to fear the judgments of God and to hate sin, which is the cause of death'.[16] The Westminster Directory for Public Worship, approved by the Scottish Parliament in 1645, reiterated this prohibition and similarly instructed that all that should happen at a burial was the placing of the body in the ground and its covering with earth, nothing more. When Queen Victoria attended a funeral at Balmoral in 1872 she noted that there was no service at all at the graveside, although the minister had said a prayer at the home of the deceased. By 1883 this had changed and at a funeral she attended that year she noted that there was a prayer at the graveside.

If the lack of a formal religious service did perhaps somewhat diminish the solemnity of Highland and Hebridean funerals, they were not without their own rituals and order. They were first and foremost spontaneous expressions of collective grief, organised and conducted by family and community without professional assistance. The often lavish provision of food and drink both before and after the burial was a way of releasing the tension and the grief and also a necessary refreshment for mourners who had often travelled a considerable distance on foot. Although both the pre- and post-burial wakes could get out of hand, they exemplified the Highland virtues of hospitality and generosity. Critical as he was when it turned to excess, Lord Teignmouth saw much to commend in what he called 'the funereal banquet in Scotland' in its 'provision of entertainment for the assembled mourners, whether terminating on the occasion itself, or prolonged for a considerable period, so as to enable all persons so disposed to pay their tribute of respect to the memory of the deceased'.

> The practice, unabused, is unobjectionable, nay necessary. The mourners are often brought from remote parts performing laborious journeys, or encountering winds and waves, to reach the place of interment, a spot frequently selected on account of its central situation, or the ancient veneration attached to it, and very far from any place of refreshment; they cannot be dismissed without it; and although the cemetery itself is unsuited for a repast, yet its immediate neighbourhood is often unavoidably chosen for the purpose. The censure belongs to the extravagance, wasteful, and sometimes ruinous: to the excess which converts the funereal banquet into a scene of mirth, disorder, and violence, and renders the serious mind of these people less susceptible of the impression of death on the very occasion of its celebration than on any other.[17]

4

Watching over the Churchyard
Morvern

The Morvern peninsula is particularly well supplied with coffin roads. It is also one of the best places to see the cairns that were erected to mark where coffins were rested. A group of them, almost covered over with long grass, was pointed out to me by Iain Thornber, the exceptionally knowledgeable historian of Morvern, on the coastal road running along the north shore of the Sound of Mull, from Drimnin to Lochaline, which formerly served as a coffin road to Kiel churchyard. They are situated beside Clach na Criche (the Boundary Stone), the outcrop of volcanic magma near Fiunary that marks the boundary between the old parishes of Killintaig and Kilcolmkiel. Another well-established coffin road crossed over the western tip of Morvern, from Bunavullin near Drimnin via Doirlinn to Laudale House on Loch Sunart, a total distance of 28 miles. It is now a Heritage Path known as the Bunavullin Coffin Roads.[1]

One of the main destinations of the Morvern coffin roads was the churchyard at Kiel (sometimes spelled Keil), which stands on a grassy hillside about a mile above the village of Lochaline, from where the ferry to Fishnish on Mull departs and where fine silica sand is extracted for use in the manufacture of high-class optical glass. The graveyard, which adjoins the church that still serves the parish of Morvern peninsula, is one of the most imposingly sited in the West Highlands, with fine views down the Sound of Mull towards Mull, Ardnamurchan and beyond to the small isles.

The graveyard at Kiel made a particular impression on one of the best-known and most influential Church of Scotland ministers of the nineteenth century, Norman MacLeod (1812–72). He was a scion of the great MacLeod dynasty who provided ministers of Morvern for an unbroken period of over a hundred years, and from whose ranks came six moderators of the General Assembly of the Church of Scotland, including George MacLeod, founder of the Iona Community. Norman MacLeod was born in Campbeltown, where his father was minister; also called Norman, MacLeod Senior was known as *Caraid nan Gaidheal* (the Friend of the Gael) because of his championship of Gaelic culture and education, and the help that he gave to West Highlanders during the period of potato famine and Clearances in the 1830s and 1840s. At the age of 12, young Norman was sent to Morvern to board with the parish schoolmaster in order to learn Gaelic and become immersed in the traditions of his ancestors. He spent a year in the parish where his uncle, John, had just become minister, having succeeded his father, Norman's grandfather. Norman MacLeod went on to serve for 20 years in the inner-city Barony Church in Glasgow, where he championed the cause of working men and initiated many social reforms, setting up loan funds and savings banks, soup kitchens and education classes. He wrote the hymn 'Courage, brother, do not stumble' and became Queen Victoria's confidant and her favourite chaplain. In common with the other ministers from this remarkable family, he combined a broad evangelical simplicity with a strong liturgical sense and an open-minded, liberal theology. In 1867 he wrote a book about the Morvern parish in which his uncle and grandfather had served and where he had spent part of his childhood, *Reminiscences of a Highland Parish*. It was republished in 2002 as *Morvern, A Highland Parish*, superbly edited by Iain Thornber. This is what MacLeod wrote there about Kiel churchyard:

> It is situated on a green plateau of table-land which forms a ledge between the low sea-shore and hilly background. A beautiful tall stone cross from Iona adorns it; a single Gothic arch of an old church remains as a witness for the once consecrated ground, and links the old 'cell' to the modern building, which in architecture – shame to modern lairds – is to the old one what a barn is to a church.
>
> The view, however, from that churchyard, of all God's glorious architecture above and below, makes one forget those paltry attempts of man to be a fellow-worker with Him in the rearing and adorning of the fitting and the beautiful. There is hardly in the Highlands a finer expanse of inland seas, of castled promontories, of hills beyond hills, until cloudland and highland mingle; of precipice and waterfall, with all the varied lights and shadows which heathy hill sides, endless hill tops, dark corries, ample bays and rocky shores, can create at morn, noonday, or evening, from sun and cloud – a glorious panorama extending from the far west beyond the giant point of Ardnamurchan, 'the height of the great ocean', to the far east, where Ben Cruachan and 'the Shepherds of Etive Glen' stand sentinels in the sky.
>
> No sea king could select a more appropriate resting-place than this, from whence to catch a glimpse, as his spirit walked abroad beneath the moonlight, of galleys coming from the Northland of his early home; nor could an old saint find a better resting-place, if he desired that

after death the mariners, struggling with stormy winds and waves, might see his cross from afar, and thence snatch comfort from this symbol of faith and hope 'in extremis'; nor could any man, who in the frailty of his human nature shrunk from burial in lonely vault, and who wished rather to lie where birds might sing, and summer's sun shine, and winter's storms lift their voices to God, and the beautiful world be ever above and around him, find a spot more congenial to his human feelings.[2]

Kiel churchyard remains today much as Norman MacLeod described it 150 years ago. The Gothic arch of its ruined medieval chapel is still there, possibly marking the site of the first ecclesiastical settlement; this may go back to the sixth or seventh century and have a link with Columba, reflected in its original name Cill Cholumchille or Kilcolmkiel. So, too, is the fine fourteenth-century carved cross which stands on the far side of a field in front of the current parish church, built in 1898 to a simple but fitting design by the great Scottish architect Peter MacGregor Chalmers, a much finer building than the barn-like structure of which MacLeod complained.

Among the many tombstones and monuments in this churchyard, the most prominent is an imposing railed-off memorial to the two MacLeods who between them clocked up over a hundred years' ministering in the parish of Morvern. The first, (another) Norman, arrived from Skye aged 30 in 1775, having been appointed by the Duke of Argyll to reconcile the many Jacobites in this northernmost part of Argyll to the final collapse of the Stuart cause and woo them from Episcopalianism to the established Presbyterian church. His command of Gaelic and strong pastoral and preaching skills won over many of his

2,000 parishioners and when he died in 1824, after 49 years in the parish, he was remembered, in the words of his memorial in the churchyard, as 'noble in appearance, excelling in scholarship, an eloquent preacher and a genial and faithful pastor'. He was succeeded as minister by his youngest son, John, who remained in the charge for 58 years until his death in 1882. Known as 'the High Priest of Morvern' partly because of his commanding physical presence– he was six feet, nine inches tall – he chose to remain in the parish throughout the period of the Clearances rather than quit it for one of the many more affluent and prestigious charges which sought to call him or emigrate with the many hundreds of his parishioners who were evicted from their crofts. The MacLeod memorial also lists the children of these long-serving ministers. Twelve of Norman MacLeod's 16 children are buried there. John's sons, Norman (1838–1911), minister of the High Church, Inverness, and John (1840–98) known as the 'Pope of Govan' for his High Church practices when he was minister there, are also commemorated on the stone.

The old session house behind the church now houses a fine collection of 17 carved medieval grave slabs. Together with the sculptured crosses similarly dating from between the fourteenth and sixteenth centuries, these were a distinctive feature of West Highland graveyards. There are over 600 of them still in existence, many now removed from their original outdoor locations and housed in sheltered buildings to protect them from wind and rain. Iona alone has over 170, many of which are displayed in the abbey museum. There are other important collections in Kilmartin churchyard, Oronsay Priory, Saddell Abbey in Kintyre and at Kilmory Knapp, Keills and Kilberry in Knapdale, mid-Argyll. With their depictions of knights in armour, bishops, abbots, highly decorated swords and galleys, they embody a very masculine, muscular Christianity – 'Courage, brother, do not stumble' indeed – and commemorate the lives, and the deaths, of the strong and powerful.

But it is not just dominant, martial men who are buried in Kiel churchyard. There are two women's graves there which particularly fascinated Norman MacLeod. A stone coffin near the ruined medieval chapel supposedly contains the body of a Spanish princess washed ashore from the *Florida*, a ship in the Spanish Armada which was fleeing up the west coast of Scotland after its routing by the English navy in 1588. It was supposedly driven into Tobermory Bay by a storm and subsequently sank there, although no wreck has been found to support this claim. MacLeod recounted the story behind this grave exactly as it was told to him by an old woman. It tells of a daughter of the king of Spain who travelled the world on a large ship, arriving eventually on Mull, where she won the heart of the Lord of Duart, who forsook his young bride for her. In revenge, the Lady of Duart set fire to the ship and blew up all those on board, including the Spanish princess, who was buried in the 'churchyard of the holy Columba (Callum Cille) in Morven, where she was committed to the dust without priest or prayer – without voice of supplication or psalm of repose – silently and secretly in the blackness of midnight'. The tale, as related to MacLeod, continues as follows:

> It chanced, shortly after this, that two young men in Morven, bound in ties of closest friendship, and freely revealing to one another all that was in their hearts, began to speak with wonder of the many great secrets of the world beyond the grave. They spoke, and they spoke of what was doing in the habitation of the spirits beyond the thick veil that hides the departed from the friends who sorrow so sorely after them. They could not see a ray of light – they could discover nothing. At length they

mutually promised and vowed, that whichever of them
was first called away would, while engaged in the dread
task of *Faire 'Chlaidh*, or 'watching of the churchyard',
tell to the survivor all that he could reveal regarding the
abode of the departed; and here the matter was left.

Not long after it fell out that one of them, full as
his bone was of marrow, yielded to the sway of death.
His body, after being carried *Deas iul* (according to
the course of the sun) around the stone cross in the
churchyard of *Callum Cille* (Columba), in Morven, and
allowed to rest for a time at the foot of that cross, was
laid amid the dust of his kindred. His surviving comrade, Evan of the Glen, mourned sore for the loss of
his friend; and much awe and fear came upon him as
he remembered the engagement made between them;
for now the autumn evening was bending (or waning),
and like a stone rolling down a hill is the faint evening
of autumn. The hour of meeting drew nigh, and regard
to the sacredness of a promise made to him who was
now in the world of ghosts, as well as regard for his
own courage, decided him to keep the tryst (meeting).
With cautious, but firm, step he approached the Cill,
and looked for his departed friend, to hear the secrets
of the land of ghosts. Quickly as his heart beat at the
thought of meeting the spirit of his friend, he soon saw
what made it quiver like the leaf of the aspen tree. He
saw the grey shade of him who had, at one time, been
his friend and his faithful comrade; but he saw all the
'sheeted spectres' of the populous churchyard moving
in mournful procession around the boundary of their
dark abodes, while his friend seemed to lead the dread
and shadowy host. But his eye was soon drawn by the

aspect of utter woe presented by one white form which kept apart from the rest, and moved with pain which cannot be told. Forgetful of what had brought him to the Cill, he drew near this sight of woe, and heard a low and most plaintive song, in which the singer implored the aid of him whose 'ship was on the ocean', bewailed her miserable condition, in a land of strangers, far from father and from friends, laid in the grave without due or holy rites, and thus she moaned:

> Worm and beetle, they are whistling
> Through my brain – through my brain;
> Imps of darkness, they are shrieking
> Through my frame – through my frame.

Evan, whose heart was ever soft and warm towards the unhappy, asked her the cause of her grief, and whether he could lighten it. She blessed him that he, in the land of the living, had spoken to her in the land of the dead; for now she said she might be freed from evil, and her spirit might rest in peace.[3]

The spectre told Evan that she was the daughter of the king of Spain and beseeched him to raise her bones, wash them in the holy well of St Moluag on Lismore and carry them back to Spain. This he duly did, although the king of Spain was so outraged when he heard how his daughter had been treated that he sent three ships to attack the three best harbours in Scotland (in the Kyles of Bute, Kerrera and Tobermory) and kill as many of the inhabitants as possible.

This story gives several insights into Highland beliefs and practices with regard to death and burial. It underlines the thin boundary that was thought to exist between the worlds of the living and the dead and the relative ease with which it could be

crossed, especially in a graveyard. It also underlines the widespread belief that the last person to be buried had the task of *Faire
'Chlaidh*. Norman MacLeod commented of this belief:

> In many parts of the Highlands it is believed to this
> day, that the last person buried has to perform the
> duty of sentinel over the churchyard, and that to him
> the guardianship of the spirits of those buried before is
> in some degree committed. This post he must occupy
> until a new tenant of the tomb releases him. It is not
> esteemed as an enviable position, but one to be escaped
> if possible; consequently, if two neighbours die on the
> same day, the surviving relatives make great efforts to be
> first in closing the grave over their friend. I remember
> an old nurse, who was mourning the death of a sweet
> girl whom she had reared, exclaiming with joy when she
> heard, on the day after her funeral, of the death of a
> parishioner, 'Thank God! My dear darling will have to
> watch the graves no longer!'[4]

Another widespread tradition mentioned in the story of the
Spanish princess is that of carrying a body *deas iul* (often spelled
deosil), i.e. sunwise or clockwise, round the churchyard. This practice continued in some Roman Catholic areas of the Highlands
and the Hebrides until well into the twentieth century. Alexander
Carmichael noted that in Tomintoul, 'the horse drawing the cart
in which a corpse is laid is taken out of the cart three times on the
journey. The horse is then turned round sunwise on the road, and
re-yoked.'[5] MacLeod offers this interesting observation on what
he describes as 'a turn the right or the south way': 'This is said to
be a Druidical practice, followed in many places to this day. Very
recently it was customary in the churchyard of the parish to carry

the bier around the stone cross which stands there, and to rest it
for a few minutes at its base before committing the body to the
grave. It is still customary with people, if any food or drink goes
wrong in the throat, to exclaim *Deas iul*, apparently as a charm,
and send the bottle round the table in the course of the sun.'[6]

A second grave in Kiel churchyard, situated on a grassy hillock
beneath the Gothic arch of the ruined chapel and next to the
stone coffin of the Spanish princess, is the subject of another fascinating story in Norman MacLeod's *Reminiscences of a Highland
Parish*, this time based on his own direct experience. It contains
the body of Flory (Flora) Cameron, a local widow accused of
being a witch but in fact a devout Christian known for her gifts
of discernment and prophecy as well as for her wild passion, and
of her three children who predeceased her. MacLeod describes
in touching detail the funeral of the last of her children to die, a
particularly beloved son. As his body was carried from her cottage
to the churchyard, Flora led the mourners, walking at the head
of the coffin and holding the black cord that was attached to it in
accordance with Highland tradition.

> The funeral procession arrived at the place of interment,
> which was only about a mile removed from her cottage.
> The grave was already dug. It extended across an old
> Gothic arch. Under it Flory sat for some moments in
> pensive silence. The coffin was placed in the grave, and
> when it had been adjusted with all due care, the attend-
> ants were about to proceed to cover it. Here, however,
> they were interrupted. Flory arose, and motioning to
> the obsequious crowd to retire, she slowly descended
> into the hollow grave, placed herself in an attitude of
> devotion, and continued for some time engaged in
> prayer to the Almighty.

The crowd of attendants had retired to a little distance, but being in some degree privileged, or at least considering myself so, I remained leaning upon a neighbouring grave-stone as near to her as I could without rudely intruding upon such great sorrow. I was however too far removed to hear distinctly the words which she uttered, especially as they were articulated in a low and murmuring tone of voice. The concluding part of her address was indeed more audibly given, and I heard her bear testimony with much solemnity to the fact that her departed son had never provoked her to wrath, and had ever obeyed her commands. She then paused for a few moments, seemingly anxious to tear herself away, but unable to do so. At length she mustered resolution, and after impressing three several kisses on the coffin, she was about to arise. But she found herself again interrupted. The clouds which had hitherto been lowering were now dispelled, and just as she was slowly ascending from the grave, the sun burst forth in full splendour from behind the dark mist that had hitherto obscured its rays. She again prostrated herself, this time under the influence of a superstitious belief still general in the Highlands, that bright sunshine upon such occasions augurs well for the future happiness of the departed. She thanked God 'that the sky was clear and serene when the child of her love was laid in the dust'. She then at length arose, and resumed her former position under the old archway, which soon re-echoed the ponderous sound of the falling earth upon the hollow coffin.

It was indeed a trying moment to her. With despair painted on her countenance, she shrieked aloud in bitter anguish, and wrung her withered hands with convulsive violence. I tried to comfort her, but she would not be comforted. In the full paroxysm of her grief, however, one of the persons in attendance approached her. 'Tears,' said her friend, 'cannot bring back the dead. It is the will of Heaven you must submit.' 'Alas!' replied Flory, 'the words of the lips are easily given, but they heal not the broken heart!' The offered consolation, however, was effectual thus far, that it recalled the mourner to herself, and led her to subdue for the time every violent emotion. She again became alive to everything around, and gave the necessary directions to those who were engaged in covering up the grave. Her directions were given with unfaltering voice, and were obeyed by the humane neighbours with unhesitating submission. On one occasion indeed, and towards the close of the obsequies, she assumed a tone of high authority. It was found that the turf which had been prepared for covering the grave was insufficient for the purpose, and one of the attendants not quite so fastidious as his countrymen, who in such cases suffer not the smallest inequality to appear, proposed that the turf should be lengthened by adding to it. The observation did not escape her notice. Flory fixed her piercing eye upon him that uttered it, and after gazing at him for some moments with bitter scorn, she indignantly exclaimed, 'Who talks of patching up the grave of my son? Get you gone and cut a green sod worthy of my beloved.' This imperative order was instantly obeyed. A suitable turf was procured, and the grave was at length covered up to the entire satisfaction of all parties. She now arose, and returned to her desolate abode, supported by two aged females, almost equally infirm with herself, and followed by her dog.[7]

MacLeod goes on to relate how, although her grief remained, Flory eventually came to terms with the cruel death of her one remaining child: 'She ceased to look for earthly comfort but found it in Christ.' She visited the grave every morning at dawn and in the evening twilight – MacLeod himself several times saw her there 'wrapped in a Highland plaid, sitting on the grave, her head bent and her hands covering her face, while her body rocked slowly to and fro', her dog sitting beside her. One morning, her neighbours, attracted by the howling of the dog and seeing no smoke from her chimney, entered her cottage unbidden and found her lying dead inside. She was laid to rest in the same grave as her children.

This poignant story reinforces the significance of the graveyard as the place to maintain contact with those who have died and in which to grieve and remember them. It also highlights other distinctive Highland beliefs, such as the importance attached both to good weather at the time of a burial and to the grave being properly covered over. Flory's own burial in the same grave as her sons underlines the compelling desire of Highlanders to be laid to rest beside their families and kindred. Norman MacLeod's reflections on this desire, which in his words almost amounted to 'a decided superstition', have already been quoted (p. 11). In his *Reminiscences*, he gives examples of the lengths to which it could be taken:

A woman from 'the mainland', somewhere in Kintail, was married to a highly respectable man in one of the Hebrides which need not be specified. When she died, twelve of her relations, strong men, armed with oak sticks, journeyed sixty miles to be present at her funeral. They quietly expressed their hope to her husband, that his wife should be buried in her own country and beside her own people. But on ascertaining from him that such was not his purpose, they declared their intention to carry off the body by force. An unseemly struggle was avoided only through the husband being unable to find any one to back him in his refusal of what was deemed by his neighbours to be a reasonable request. He therefore consented, and accompanied the body to the churchyard of her family.

This feeling is carried to a length which, in one instance I have heard of, was too ludicrous to be dignified even by the name of superstition. A Highland porter, who carried our bag but the other day, and who has resided for thirty years in the low country, sent his amputated finger to be buried in the graveyard of the parish beside the remains of his kindred! It is said that a bottle of whisky was sent along with the finger that it might be entombed with all honour!

This desire of being interred with kindred dust or with 'the faithful ones', as they express it, is so strong, that I have known a poor man selling all his potatoes, and reducing himself to great suffering, in order to pay the expense of burying his wife in a distant churchyard among her people; and that, too, when the minister of his parish offered to bury her at his own expense in the churchyard of the parish in which the widower resided. Only a year or two ago a pauper in the parish of K begged another poor neighbour to see her buried beside her family. When she died, twelve men assembled, carried her ten miles off, dug her grave, and paid all the expenses of her funeral, which, had she been buried elsewhere, would have been paid by the parish.[8]

Norman MacLeod has been quoted a good deal in this chapter because he is surely the most eloquent and perceptive commentator on the Hebridean and Highland graveyards, of which Kiel in Morvern is such a fine example. He was moved by its particular atmosphere and 'picturesque' quality to make this more general observation:

Many of those Highland churchyards, so solitary and so far removed from the busy haunts of men, are, nevertheless, singularly touching and beautiful. Some are on green islands whose silence is disturbed only by the solemn thunder of the great ocean wave, or the ripple of the inland sea; some are in great wide glens, among bracken and blooming heather, round the ruins of a chapel, where prayers were once offered by early missionaries, who with noble aim and holy ambition penetrated these wild and savage haunts; while others break the green swards about the parish church on ground where God has been worshipped since the days of St Columba.

The Highland churchyard is a spot which seldom betrays any other traces of human art or care than those simple headstones which mark its green graves. In very few instances is it enclosed; its graves generally mingle with the mountain pasture and blooming heather, and afford shelter to the sheep and lamb from the blast of winter and the heat of summer. But although not consecrated by holy prayer and religious ceremony, these are, nevertheless, holy spots in the hearts and memories of the peasantry, who never pass them without a subdued look, which betokens a feeling of respect for the silent sleepers. To deck a father's or mother's grave, would be, in the estimation of the Highlander, to turn it into a flower-garden. He thinks it utter vanity to attempt to express his grief or respect for the departed by any ornament beyond the tombstone, whose inscription is seldom more than a statistical table of birth and death.[9]

In fact, as we shall see in the next chapter, Highland gravestones do quite often display more than just a bare statistical record of dates of birth and death. On many of them there is a stark *memento mori*, or reminder of death, in the form either of a carved symbol or a brief epithet or poem. But MacLeod was right to emphasise their simple and unadorned character. There are no weeping angels, cherubs or statuettes, no posies or bowls of flowers, either real or artificial. Some visitors find Highland graveyards unkempt and untidy and compare them unfavourably to the manicured lawns and symmetrically aligned rows of headstones in urban cemeteries. But they are in a minority. Most sense the beauty and authenticity behind their simplicity and closeness to nature. They are part of a wild and natural landscape in which death has not been tamed or prettified but where it is acknowledged and integrated. They are places where one can face death and contemplate eternity with equanimity, nowhere more so, in my experience, than while sitting among the tussocks and stones in Kiel graveyard.

5

Islands of Graves
The Green Isle, Loch Shiel

The final destination of a number of coffin roads going through Ardnamurchan, Sunart and Moidart – that most mysterious and remote part of the West Highlands – is for me the most haunting island graveyard anywhere in Scotland. Eilean Fhianain (St Finnan's Isle), also known as the Green Isle, in Loch Shiel, is possibly the oldest burial ground in western Europe still in use today. The county boundary between Argyll and Inverness for long ran down the middle of the island, which is now wholly in Inverness. Protestants from Sunart and Ardgour were buried on its southern slopes and Catholics from Moidart on the northern side. The island takes its name from the seventh-century Irish saint, Finnan, who is said to have landed at Kilchoan and then walked across the Ardnamurchan peninsula, stopping to rest on the shoulder of a hill, known as Suidhe Fhianain (St Finnan's Seat), between the townships of Ockle and Gortenfern. From there he saw the island on which he resolved to establish a hermitage where he is said to have lived for some years. Burials are thought to have begun on the island in his time, or possibly earlier, and it has been claimed, rather fancifully, that since then there have been around 60,000 interments. Father William Fraser, for many years the local Roman Catholic parish priest, told me that it was very difficult when digging a new grave to find a piece of ground that was not already full of bones.

Several coffin roads converge on the jetty at Port Nan Eilein on the north side of Loch Shiel, from which bodies were conveyed to the Green Isle. One of the longest starts at Glenuig on the north-west tip of Moidart and followed the line now taken by the road that goes along the north side of Loch Moidart. A war memorial, erected in 2014 in memory of those from Moidart who died in the First and Second World Wars, stands beside a coffin cairn on this route on the west side of the road, about two miles south of Glenuig. Another coffin road, which is essentially an extension of the one from Glenuig, runs from Dalilea (sometimes referred to as Dalelia) to the jetty at Port Nan Eilein. Featured on the 'Wild About Lochaber' website, it provides a pleasant short walk through fields and woods, passing both a Bronze Age burial cairn and a large cross erected by the local landowner, Lord Howard Glossop, in memory of his son, who was killed in the First World War. The jetty at Port Nan Eilein is still used for transporting bodies to the Green Isle. There is another jetty near Achnanellan on the south side of Loch Shiel, which was the embarkation point for bodies conveyed along coffin roads through Sunart and Ardgour.

I am not alone in being captivated by the atmosphere of the Green Isle. Norman MacLeod described it as one of the most beautiful Highland graveyards that he had ever visited. He gives this lyrical account of how he reached it and what he found there:

> The loch for nearly twenty miles is as yet innocent of roads on either shore, so that the tourist who visits the place has to navigate the lake in a rude country boat; and if he attempts to sail, he must probably do so with blankets attached to the oar, and then trust to a fair

wind. Yet what can be more delicious than thus to glide along the shore with a crew that won't speak till they are spoken to, and in silence gaze upon the ever-varying scene – to skim past the bights and bays with their reedy margins – the headlands tufted with waving birch – the gulfy torrents pouring down their foaming waterfalls and 'blowing their trumpets from the steeps' with the copse of oak and hazel, that covers the sides of the mountain from the deep dark water up to the green pasture, and beyond, the bare rocks that pierce the blue.

Not unlikely the crew, when they take to their oars, will sing 'Ho Mhorag', in honour of Prince Charlie, 'the lad wi' the philabeg', who on the green diluvial plain at the head of the loch where his monument now stands first unfurled his banner, to regain the British crown; and if you don't know this romantic episode in history, the boatmen will point out with pride the glens where the Camerons, Macdonalds, Stewarts, and Macleans poured down their kilted clans, the last 'old guard' of the clan times, to do battle for 'the yellow-haired laddie'; and unless you cordially believe (at least until you leave Loch Shiel) that you would have joined them on that day, with the probability even of losing your head and your common sense, you are not in a fit state of spirit to enjoy the scene.

Halfway up this lake, and at its narrowest portion, there is a beautiful green island, which stretches itself so far across as to leave but a narrow passage for even the country boat. Above it, and looking down on it, rises Ben Reshiepol for 2,000 feet or more, with its hanging woods, grey rocks, dashing streams, and utter solitude. On the island is an old chapel, with the bell, now we believe preserved by the laird, which long ago so often broke the silence of these wilds on holy days of worship or of burial. There lie chiefs and vassals, fierce cateran robbers of sheep and cattle, murderers of opposing clans, with women and children, Catholic and Protestant, Prince Charlie men, and men who served in army and navy under George the Third.

How silent is the graveyard! You sit down among the ruins and hear only the bleat of sheep, the whish-whish of the distant waterfalls, the lapping of the waves, or the wind creeping through the archways and mouldering windows. The feuds and combats of the clans are all gone; the stillness and desolation of their graves alone remain.[1]

I have to confess that I dismally failed MacLeod's test for being in a fit state to enjoy the scene when I made my own trip to the island one beautiful summer morning in a boat from Acharacle. My strong Campbell genes meant that I was not possessed of any desire to join the Jacobite rebellion. Nor were there any blanketed oars or singing to accompany me, just the steady throb of an outboard engine and the companionship of a taciturn boatman who left me to explore the island on my own for two or three hours. I found its atmosphere both haunting and utterly absorbing. The grassy slopes are almost completely covered with stone graves and crosses, some very ancient and now at crazy angles, all pointing towards the sky. Scrub and undergrowth have been cleared away, making the island easy to walk over.

At the highest point of the island is the small ruined chapel of St Finnan. Until it was stolen in 2019, an ancient bell was housed in a recess behind the altar on the east wall. Although reputedly used by Finnan, it is unlikely that it dated back beyond

the tenth century. The bell was said to be heard ringing sometimes by those fishing in the loch even when there was no one
on the island. In her book on *Music and the Celtic Otherworld*,
Karen Ralls-MacLeod notes that in the lives of Celtic saints, 'we
often see examples of a tongueless bell sounding on its own, this
miracle of God reflecting the otherworldly status of the Christian
heaven'.[2] Along with trumpets and harps, bells are among the
instruments most associated with the sound and music of heaven.
Standing alone in the ruined chapel, it is not difficult to imagine
St Finnan's bell being rung of an evening by one of the spirits on
this island of the dead. It is much to be hoped that it will either
be recovered or replaced before too long.

We have already noted the popularity of islands in the western
sea as places of burial and the significance in Celtic mythology,
drawing on Ancient Greek ideas, of the isles of the blessed, the
isles of the saints, the islands of promise and the isles beneath the
waves. Inland lochs had their own place in the Celtic imagination
and were also associated with death. Their islands, too, became
favoured places on which to be buried. In part, this was because
of the frequent representation of dying as involving crossing over
water. This has been understood both metaphorically and literally by different cultures and religions. It is, of course, a strong
theme in Greek mythology where the souls of the newly dead
were rowed by the ferryman, Charon, across the River Styx which
encircled the underworld and formed the boundary between the
worlds of the living and the dead. The Buddha is often portrayed
in similar terms as a ferryman and one of his discourses compares
monks crossing Mara's stream to make the journey from life to
death to cattle crossing the River Ganga and arriving safe on the
further shore. Within Christianity, a similar idea is powerfully
represented in the image of crossing the River Jordan, found in
John Bunyan's classic *The Pilgrim's Progress*, when Christian and

Hopeful have to wade through a deep river to reach the celestial city, and in African-American spirituals like 'Deep river, my
home is over Jordan'.

Among many primal peoples the dead are believed to cross
rivers or lakes to enter the next world. The Yoruba people of
Nigeria bury their dead in canoes to prepare them for their journey
across one or more rivers to enter the next world. Members of the
Wägilak clan, living in the remote community of Ngukurr on the
Roper River in Arnhem Land in Australia's Northern Territory,
believe that each individual's life is a thread woven into a much
bigger ongoing string or *raki* into which it is absorbed at death.
The souls of the departed join their ancestors by being symbolically pulled into the deep waters of Blue Mud Bay by a harpoon
string as their names are intoned in song. The early Vikings often
buried their dead either in ships, as in Oslo fjord, or in graves
designed in the shape of ships, as on the island of Lau in Gotland,
Sweden, to symbolise the journey of death. A Viking boat burial
from the ninth or tenth century was discovered and excavated in
1882 on the sand dunes of Kiloran Bay, on the north-west coast
of Colonsay. It consisted of an overturned boat, at least 30 feet
in length, covering the body of a man in a crouched position
who had been buried together with a sword, spearhead, axehead,
shield, knife, two arrowheads, various tools and ornaments and a
set of weighing scales with weights and measures. Buried next to
him was a horse. The whole structure was covered by a mound of
sand and at either end of it were two slabs, each roughly carved
with a Christian cross, suggesting that the practice of boat burials
did not end with the coming of Christianity.

The symbol of the birlinn, or sea-going galley, perhaps appears
on so many Hebridean and West Highland grave slabs because
it, too, symbolises the journey of death and represents it as
a pilgrimage across water. It has certainly had this meaning in

folklore and among mystics. Niall, the 10th Duke of Argyll, who was much given to mystical experiences and regularly communed with fairies in the grounds of Inveraray Castle, had visions of the Galley of Lorne crewed by the spirits of his ancestors passing over Loch Fyne on its journey to the original Campbell heartland of Loch Awe. Ancient Egyptians experienced similar visions, in which recently dead pharaohs were seen sailing across the sky on a reed raft or wooden boat steered by a helmsman who always looked backwards.

Many near-death experiences involve either floating on or being absorbed into water, and there is a vast corpus of literature from many different traditions envisaging death as being like a river or stream flowing out into a lake or sea.[3] Maybe this imagery about crossing rivers and lakes partly explains the attraction of burial on islands in inland lochs. There is also the proximity of running water, which allows spirits to escape, a factor which we have already noted with regard to the siting of Highland and Hebridean graveyards near fast-flowing streams. The comparative remoteness, tranquillity and peace of island graveyards undoubtedly also added to their appeal.

The Green Isle on Loch Shiel is by no means the only popular burial ground situated on an island in the middle of a loch. Alexander Ewing, who in 1847 was consecrated as the first bishop of the newly united diocese of Argyll and the Isles in the Scottish Episcopal Church, was fascinated by the appeal of Eilean Munde in Loch Leven just north of Ballachulish, which although properly speaking a sea loch is almost entirely surrounded by land, with only a narrow channel out to Loch Linnhe under the Ballachulish Bridge. The earliest burials there seem to have been of those converted to Christianity by St Munn, like Finnan an Irish saint, from Leinster, who is said to have spent some time living as a hermit on the island. Although he himself was probably buried at

Burial cists in Temple Wood, Kilmartin Valley.

Ballymeanoch standing stones, Kilmartin Valley.

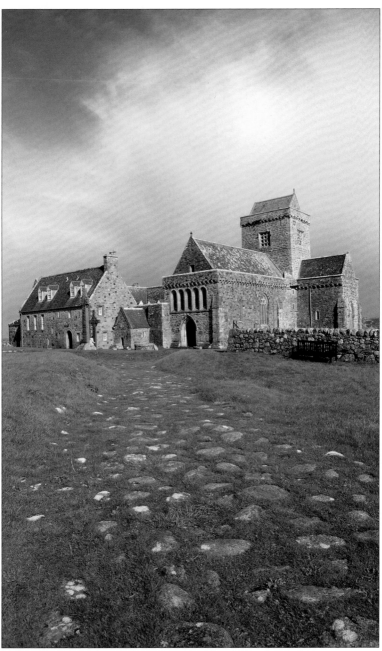

Street of the Dead, Iona. (UK Rural Images Scotland/Alamy Stock Photo)

Kilearnadil Graveyard, Jura. (Jaime Pharr/Alamy Stock Photo)

Cairns on Morvern coffin road.

Kiel cemetery, Morvern.

Green Isle, Loch Shiel.

Ancient gravestones on Green Isle.

St Finan's bell, Green Isle.

Memento mori – skull, crossbones, hourglass and trumpet on gravestone in Kiel cemetery.

Piper's Cairn, Eigg. (Kumar Sriskandan/Alamy Stock Photo)

Kintail coffin road. (Heritage Paths)

Barra coffin road. (Heritage Paths. Copyright Becky Williamson)

St Brendan's Church, Craigston, Barra. (Roman Catholic Diocese of Argyll)

St Brendan's Church burial ground, Borve, Barra.
(Alan Pateman-Jones / Commonwealth War Graves Commission)

Skeleton grave on Green Isle.

Kilmun, near Dalavich on Loch Awe, many of his followers seem
to have wanted to lie near his cell on Eilean Munde. It became the
favoured burial place for several branches of the MacDonald clan,
somewhat surprisingly, given that Munn was closely associated
with the Campbells and effectively taken up as their patron saint.
Bishop Ewing was amazed to discover on a visit to the island in
1872 that it was still much sought after as a final resting place,
not least by people from as far afield as the United States, who
sometimes came over while they were still alive to 'await their end
near the venerable churchyard'. He met one elderly American
who had arrived in Ballachulish close to death but subsequently
recovered his health and was uncertain what to do next.[4]

There is another inland island graveyard which I find very
atmospheric. Inishail, also known as the Island of Rest or the
Green Isle, lies in the northern part of Loch Awe. Its graveyard is
reached by taking a small boat – in my case from Ardbrecknish
near Cladich – to a little beach on the west side of the thickly
wooded island, and clambering up through dank vegetation to
the yew trees spreading their dark pall over a ruined chapel which
may possibly stand on the site of a nunnery founded by Findoca.
It has been suggested that early Campbell chiefs were buried here
before the building of the collegiate church at Kilmun on the
Holy Loch, but there is no evidence for this and it seems more
likely that they were laid to rest at the other Kilmun close to
Davalich and overlooking the old Campbell stronghold of Innis
Chonell further down Loch Awe. Later Campbell chiefs, the earls
and dukes of Argyll, were buried at Kilmun on the Holy Loch,
initially under the floor of the parish church and from the 1790s
in the specially constructed mausoleum next to it. It was here that
what was perhaps the last great burial of a Highland chieftain
took place, in May 1914, when the body of John, the 9th Duke
of Argyll, was laid to rest. More than 9,000 people had travelled

from as far afield as the Western Isles, Tiree, Iona and Lismore, to line the banks of the Holy Loch as his coffin was landed from a steamer at Kilmun pier. A pipe band led the procession that climbed up the hill to the churchyard and the family accompanied the coffin into the cold mausoleum.

Some 46 years before his death, while he was still Marquess of Lorne, John Campbell had been much affected by a visit to another island graveyard, telling his mother, 'I have been wandering where "the wild river fed from the hills of Ben More encircles the island of graves". There is certainly no place like it – and one feels as if the rush of the waters on either side were a *coronach* (lament) to be wailed by them for ever.'⁵ This was the tiny island of Inchbuie, or Innis Bhuide, in the middle of the River Dochart just down from the Falls of Dochart at Killin, which was the ancient burial place of the MacNab clan and of their chiefs. The description of 'the island of graves' that he quoted comes from a poem entitled 'The Burial Place of the Macnabs' by Francis Egerton, 1st Earl of Ellesmere. One wonders if the 9th Duke of Argyll would have liked an island grave himself rather than interment in the Argyll mausoleum at Kilmun, whose gloomy atmosphere troubled him when he first visited it and prompted him to instal a cast-iron dome with 12 skylights to make the interior more light and airy. In fact, that boon has been granted to the two most recently deceased dukes of Argyll whose remains lie in the graveyard on Inishail. It is said that the 11th duke, who died in 1973, did not want to lie with his forebears in the Argyll mausoleum at Kilmun because of its proximity to the Polaris nuclear submarine base then located in the Holy Loch. So his ashes were interred on Inishail where his father, Walter Campbell, a grandson of the 8th duke, was already buried. He is commemorated by a high-standing Celtic cross. The 12th duke, who died in 2001, is buried in a railed enclosure in long grass beyond the graveyard. His massive tombstone, with his name Ian engraved in large letters below a boar's head, is already overgrown and looks somewhat forlorn, a reminder that even the mighty MacCailean Mór is mortal.

Inishail has a number of elaborately carved grave slabs showing effigies of knights in full armour as well as many simple stones commemorating those who did not achieve such power or emi- nence and which often do not even have a name on them. It also has its fair share of gravestones on which are carved stark and chilling symbols of mortality, usually in the form of either an hourglass, a trumpet (to sound the last trump), the scythe of the Grim Reaper, or a skull and crossbones, or sometimes all five together. These symbols are particularly prevalent throughout West Highland graveyards – Kiel in Morvern has a profusion of them. Other gravestones simply have the words *memento mori* engraved on them. Travellers to the region have long commented on this feature of its landscape. After visiting Glenorchy Church in Dalmally in 1819, the poet Robert Southey observed that 'it seems the custom to engrave skulls, and other such hideous emblems of mortality upon tombstones'. He also commented that 'a great proportion of the gravestones bear the name Campbell'.[6] On her tramps through the West Highlands more than a hundred years later, the intrepid traveller and writer Mary Donaldson was simi- larly struck by the popularity of the skull and crossbones device on gravestones and suggested somewhat mischievously that it was 'more suitable, surely, for marking the graves of pirates or pagans than of professing Christians!'[7]

These grim symbols are sometimes accompanied by verses reminding those who stop to read them of their own mortality. An early eighteenth-century table tomb in Kilmun churchyard has a Gaelic verse which, when translated, reads: 'As long as you are alive, before your body becomes cold, frequently remember

death'. Inscribed on a gravestone in Kilmartin churchyard commemorating Elizabeth McFarlane, who died in 1809, are the
words:

> It is God that lifts our comforts high
> Or sinks them in the grave
> He gives and then he takes away
> He takes but what he gave

Perhaps most pointed of all is the verse under a carving of
an hourglass on the back of a gravestone in Kilfinan churchyard
on the west side of the Cowal peninsula which commemorates
Duncan Thomson, who died at the age of 52 in 1814:

> My glass is run
> And yours is running
> Be wise in time
> Your day is coming

No other part of the British Isles, or indeed of Scotland, has
such a concentration of these macabre symbols and verses. Why
is this? In a booklet that she wrote about Kilberry Church, the
Argyll historian and author Marion Campbell suggests that it
is because they were all that was allowed on gravestones after
the Reformation. But that would surely apply to the rest of the
country and does not explain the exceptional emphasis on both
the imminence and the cold reality of death in West Highland
graveyards. Is it, I wonder, another aspect of the Highlander's
openness to death and resolve to face it square on and not hide
or soften it? The ubiquity of these symbols of the hourglass,
trumpet, scythe and skull and crossbones could be taken as an
indication of just how seriously and solemnly death was regarded.

On the other hand, I suppose it could equally well be argued that, like the cautionary verses, they were there to alert and maybe even frighten a people who were regarded as being too relaxed about the subject.

Not all the inscriptions in West Highland graveyards are quite so sombre. There is a rather delightful one on a stone in the small circular cemetery at Lochead at the head of Loch Caolisport in South Knapdale. Commemorating Donald MacEachern, the local minister who died suddenly at the age of 48 on his way from the manse to conduct Sunday worship in the little church at Achahoish, it reads: 'Absent from the body. At home with the Lord where congregations ne'er break up and Sabbaths have no end.' These graphic and moving symbols and inscriptions form an important part of the Highland landscape of death, acknowledging its physical reality and finality as well as its spiritual dimension and promise of resurrection and immortality. Near the summit of the Green Isle a particularly realistic-looking skeleton is carved on the top of a recumbent tombstone. It provides an unequivocal reminder of the fate that awaits us all before we finally return ashes to ashes and dust to dust. Yet it does this without being gloomy or spooky, suggesting rather that we will merge into the green, green grass and find our natural place as well as our rest there.

6

Death Croons and Soul Leadings
The Piper's Cairn, Eigg

Among the main tourist attractions recommended to visitors to the island of Eigg is a substantial pile of stones beside the moorland track that leads across the south side of the island from the deserted township of Grulin, from where 13 families were evicted during the Clearances, to the ferry terminal at Galmisdale and eventually on to the churchyard at Kildonnan, a rare example of a coffin road running from west to east. It is known locally as 'the Piper's Cairn' and marks the place where bearers of the coffin of Donald MacQuarrie, *An Pìobair Mòr* or the 'Great Piper of Eigg', rested on the way to Kildonnan churchyard. MacQuarrie, who lived in the later eighteenth century and studied at the famous MacCrimmon piping school near Dunvegan on Skye, had probably often played his pipes on the coffin road between Grulin and Kildonnan before making his final journey along it.

Bagpipes were regularly played at Highland and Hebridean funerals although the clergy disapproved of the practice, which they associated with carousing and drinking. In his notes to Norman MacLeod's *Reminiscences of a Highland Parish*, Iain Thornber mentions a funeral where one piper who had indulged too freely in liquor failed to play the expected lament and instead struck up the jaunty dance tune 'Calum Crubach' (Lame

Callum). He also notes that mourners at a funeral in Lochaber were so upset by the piper's playing that one of them stuck his dirk into the windbag to stop the music. The practice of playing the pipes at funerals, and at the processions along the coffin roads that preceded them, became less widespread from the middle of the nineteenth century. As early as 1836 Lord Teignmouth reported being told regretfully by Highlanders of 'the cessation of the bagpipe at funerals' and noted: 'In Scotland the dance has been discontinued and the bagpipe is no longer used at funerals'.[1]

The spreading influence of the Free Church through much of the Highlands and Islands following the Disruption of 1843 undoubtedly curbed the use of bagpipes at funerals but the practice did not entirely die out. Norman MacLeod described the funeral in the mid 1860s of a much loved doctor in Fort William who had contracted typhus from one of his patients. It was attended by around 1,400 mourners. Three pipers headed the funeral procession to the burial ground at Kilmallie near Corpach, playing the wild and sad lament, 'I'll never, I'll never, I'll never return'.[2]

If Donald MacQuarrie, the piper, was Eigg's most famous late eighteenth-century resident, then its best-known late nineteenth-century son was Kenneth Macleod, born on the island in 1871, who went on to be parish minister first of Colonsay and Oronsay from 1917 to 1923 and then of Gigha and Cara until 1947. He died in 1955, is buried in Taynuilt cemetery and commemorated in stained-glass windows in both Gigha Parish Church and Iona Abbey. He is remembered primarily as a collector of folklore, being responsible with Marjory Kennedy-Fraser for the three-volume *Songs of the Hebrides*, and as the author of the song 'The Road to the Isles'. Among the traditional songs that he collected from his native Eigg were several versions of the death croon (which he calls *An Cronan Bais*), which was chanted over the dying. Macleod wrote about the origins and development of this distinctive feature of the Hebridean approach to death and dying in the first volume of *Songs of the Hebrides*, published in 1909:

> In the days of the old Celtic church, the Death-croon was chanted over the dying by the *anam-chara*, the soul friend, assisted by three chanters. Later on, the rite passed into the hands of *seanairean a' bhaile*, the elders of the township, and the *mnathan-tuiridh*, the mourning women, the latter eventually developing into a professional class, whose services could always be obtained for a consideration. In more recent times, the *bean-ghluin*, the knee-woman, or midwife, was also the *bean-tuiridh*, the mourning woman, and as the friend of the folk in the coming and the going of life, was regarded with the greatest veneration both by young and by old. To this day the knee-woman of the isles chants her runes and celebrates her mysteries in the houses of birth and of death, but always with closed doors – metaphorically, at any rate.[3]

This fascinating description takes us back to the role of the *anamchara*, or soul friend, in early Celtic Christianity. Essentially a feature of the monastic nature of the early Irish (and therefore Scottish) Church, soul friendship provided every monk with an *anamchara*, not necessarily ordained, who combined the roles of cell-mate, confessor, buddy, spiritual director and companion. It is difficult to discern how much the figure of the *anamchara* was found outside the bounds of the monastic ditch or *vallum*, although it is clear that lay people, especially kings and nobles, did also have soul friends. Particular value was placed on having your soul friend present at the time of your death.[4]

It is clear from what Kenneth Macleod writes that the *anam-chara*'s role of being present at the time of death had passed to a semi-professional class of mourning women, who often doubled as midwives, and who were brought into the houses of the dying to sing the death croon over them and so assist their souls on their journey into the next life. In the *Songs of the Hebrides* he includes this death croon that he learned partly from his aunt and partly from another long time native of Eigg:

> Home thou'rt going tonight to the winter ever-house,
> The autumn, summer, and springtide ever-house,
> Home thou art going tonight on music of cantors,
> White angels thee wait on the shores of the river.
> God the Father with thee in sleep,
> Jesus Christ with thee in sleep,
> God the spirit with thee in sleep,
> Softly sleep, softly sleep.
> Sleep oh love on mother's bosom,
> Sleep while she sings soft lullings to thee,
> The sleep of the Son on Mary's bosom,
> Sleep and put off from thee every woe.[5]

Macleod quotes another death croon, which he said was chanted over a dying person on the island of Eigg in 1890:

> The mist the dew,
> The dew the mist,
> The mist the dew
> In the eye of my love,
> In the eye of my love.
> Thou who did'st open the young eye,
> Close it tonight in the sleep of death.[6]

Providing an indication of just how long the tradition of the death croon had existed on Eigg, he also quoted an extract from one which was supposedly chanted over the grave of St Donnan, beheaded on the island in 617 along with 50 of his monks apparently on the orders of a pagan Pictish queen. The chanting was heard at midnight, when Donnan and his fellow martyrs were 'sleeping their first night's death sleep', at the same time as a blessed bright light was seen above their graves.

> Early gives the sun greeting to Donnan,
> Early sings the bird the greatness of Donnan,
> Early grows the grass on the grave of Donnan,
> The warm eye of Christ on the grave,
> The stars of the heavens on the grave,
> No harm, no harm to Donnan's dust.[7]

Death croons were not always in the form of blessings; they could also be malevolent. Macleod quotes one that was crooned by three wizards over a man 'in the death throe' standing beside a dark black loch among the hills, a location which, according to Macleod, in the isles 'is always associated with death and unholy deeds and croons'. A clergyman who happened to be passing the loch, and who witnessed this scene as if in a terrifying vision, made a caim, or sacred circle, around himself to counteract the power of the croon.[8]

Another story recounted by Kenneth Macleod, set in a Highland village at the time of reprisals following the 1745 Jacobite rising and the Battle of Culloden, further underlines the ambiguity of the death croon and the way it could be sung with either a benevolent or malevolent intention. Translated from the Gaelic by the late Catherine MacKinven for Alastair McIntosh and quoted in his book *Poacher's Pilgrimage*, it describes the death of an English redcoat officer who fell off a cliff while searching for hidden treasure. His commander knew of the tradition of singing *tuireadh*, or elegiac laments, over the dead and called on the three local mourning women to perform the ritual. They came and although they had tears in their eyes, the song that they sang in Gaelic expressed delight that the Englishman had departed and hope that his companions would go the same way. The commander, who did not understand Gaelic, thanked them for their lament and rewarded each of them with a silver coin.

As the women departed, they were struck with remorse. They had liked the English officer even if they hated what he represented and they felt it was quite wrong to have left him without a *tàladh* or death lullaby. They hastened back to the big house where his body was laid out. One of the women, who was gifted with the second sight, discerned that his soul had not yet left his body. Sitting by his bed, they sang together slowly and softly a version of the death croon about going home to the everlasting house of winter, autumn, summer and spring. The story goes on: 'His eyes were closed, the door of the soul was opened, his spirit took the road of the fathers to the sea and to the other side of the horizon.' The first woman then announced that she would make a *bonnach* (scone) to keep him going on his journey, the second prepared a lantern to light his way, and the third resolved to take the three coins that they had been given by the commander and fashion from them 'a key that will open the door of Paradise for our beloved man'. It is a story which, as Alastair McIntosh notes, borrowing from J.M. Barrie's *Rectorial Address at St Andrews University* in 1922, speaks of redemption where 'beauty boils over and the spiral of violence is thrust into reverse'. It is also a powerful encapsulation of the Highland and Hebridean understanding of how the soul leaves the body, taken to the sea and the ancestors, and the key role of the chanting of the death croon in aiding its journey.[9]

There is another interesting dimension to this story. The

intuition of the woman gifted with second sight that the soul of the English officer had not left his body could be taken to indicate something close to the Zoroastrian belief that the soul does not leave the body at the moment of death but rather hovers in the vicinity for some days before beginning its journey to the afterlife. In Zoroastrian tradition the soul stays close to the body, meditating on the life it has lived for three nights. On the first night it reflects on its words; on the second on its thoughts; and on the third on its deeds. Not until the fourth day does it set off into the afterlife. The Hebridean tradition of keeping the dead in the house for two or three days and nights might suggest a similar belief, although it should be said that references to souls lingering after death, as here, are very few and far between.

Another late nineteenth-century Hebridean folklorist with an island upbringing was also fascinated by the tradition of the death croon, or the death blessing as he called it. Alexander Carmichael, born in 1832 on the island of Lismore, transcribed and collected several such blessings while working as an exciseman in the Outer Isles, and later published them in English translations in his *Carmina Gadelica*. Like Macleod, he noted how the figure of the *anamchara*, familiar in early Celtic Christianity, had developed into a specialised form of lay ministry to the dying which was still very much in existence in the Hebrides in his own time:

> Death blessings vary in words but not in spirit. They are known by various names, such as *Beannachadh Bais* (Death Blessing), *Treoraich Anama* (Soul Leading), *Fois Anama* (Soul Peace), and others familiar to the people.
>
> The soul peace is intoned, not necessarily by a cleric, over the dying, and the man or the woman who says it is called *anam-chara* (soul friend). He or she is held in special affection by the friends of the dying person ever

after. The soul peace is slowly sung – all present earnestly joining the soul friend in beseeching the Three Persons of the Godhead and all the saints of heaven to receive the departing soul of earth. During the prayer the soul friend makes the sign of the cross with the right thumb over the lips of the dying.

The scene is touching and striking in the extreme, and the man or woman is not to be envied who could witness unmoved the distress of these lovable people of the West taking leave of those who are near and dear to them in their pilgrimage, as they say, of crossing *abhuinn dubh a bhais* (the black river of death), *cuan mor na duibhre* (the great ocean of darkness), and *beanntaibh na bith-bhuantachd* (the mountains of eternity). The scene may be in a lowly cot begrimed with smoke and black with age, but the heart is not less warm, the tear is not less bitter, and the parting is not less distressful, than in the court of the noble or in the palace of royalty.[10]

Carmichael goes on to note that the death blessings and soul leadings were chanted with the purpose of speeding the dying person on his or her pilgrimage. At the moment of death, when 'the soul is seen ascending like a bright ball of light into the clouds', those present join the *anamchara* in saying:

The poor soul is now set free
Outside the soul shrine;
O kindly Christ of the three blessings
Encompass thou my love in thine.[11]

Carmichael collected a number of death blessings from crofters and fishing communities in the Western Isles. One, which he came across in several versions on the island of Lewis, is very similar to the death croon that Kenneth Macleod learned on Eigg:

> Thou goest home this night to thy home of winter,
> To thy home of autumn, of spring, and of summer;
> Thou goest home this night to thy perpetual home,
> To thine eternal bed, to thine eternal slumber.
>
> Sleep thou, sleep, and away with thy sorrow,
> Sleep thou, sleep, and away with thy sorrow,
> Sleep thou, sleep, and away with thy sorrow;
> Sleep, thou beloved, in the Rock of the fold.
>
> Sleep this night in the breast of thy Mother,
> Sleep, thou beloved, while she herself soothes thee;
> Sleep thou this night on the Virgin's arm,
> Sleep, thou beloved, while she herself kisses thee.
>
> The great sleep of Jesus, the surpassing sleep of Jesus,
> The sleep of Jesus' wound, the sleep of Jesus' grief.
> The young sleep of Jesus, the restoring sleep of Jesus,
> The sleep of the kiss of Jesus of peace and of glory.[12]

Prominent here is the idea of death as a long and deep sleep in which sorrow is banished and also as a coming home. Jesus and the Virgin Mary are both invoked and seen as close and soothing presences. Another soul leading collected by Carmichael invokes the Archangel Michael, chief of all the angels and a figure much mentioned in poems, prayers and on gravestones in the West Highlands:

> And be the holy Michael, king of angels,
> Coming to meet the soul,

And leading it home
To the heaven of the Son of God.
The Holy Michael, high king of angels,
Coming to meet the soul,
And leading it home
To the heaven of the Son of God.[13]

The image presented here of the Archangel Michael coming to meet the dying soul and leading it home to heaven recalls Adomnán's description of the angels coming to meet the holy soul of Columba (p. 37). A similar sense of saints and angels welcoming the soul as it embarks on the journey of death, likened to the crossing of a river, is conveyed in this blessing:

Be each saint in heaven,
Each sainted woman in heaven,
Each Angel in heaven,
Stretching their arms for you,
Smoothing the way for you,
When you go thither
Over the river hard to see,
When you go thither home
Over the river hard to see.[14]

Another rather beautiful image occurs in a rhyme that Carmichael heard Hebridean children singing in which a golden butterfly is seen as an angel of God sent to bear the souls of the dead to heaven:

Butterfly! Butterfly!
Whose the soul thou didst bear,
Butterfly! Butterfly!
Yesterday to heaven?

In his notes about this rhyme, Carmichael writes: 'if the Yellow Butterfly be seen in a home where lies a corpse, and if it goes across the corpse in the chest of sleep (coffin) or upon the bier, the soul of that corpse is safe in heaven. This is not true of all, but only of the Yellow Butterfly.' He quotes a crofter from Benbecula, John MacRury:

> Tradition says that there was never a Yellow Butterfly on earth until Christ came forth from death and rose up from the tomb. The true Yellow Butterfly, they say, came out of the Holy Tomb, and that Yellow Butterfly spread throughout the world. The true Yellow Butterfly was never seen among wicked men, among evil company, evil speech, evil deeds, things hateful, things shameful, things vicious.
>
> It is a good sign to see the Yellow Butterfly upon a corpse or near a corpse. They say that every furrow and streak in his wings and in his head and in his body is exactly in the manner of those that were in the sacred corpse and body of the Saviour lying in the linen shroud.[15]

It is interesting to note here that the Slavs of Bulgaria believed that the soul of a dying person took wing as a butterfly which lingered to witness its own obsequies before flying off to the land of death.

The idea that singing or chanting over the dying aided their passage to the next world is not peculiar to the inhabitants of the Scottish Highlands and Islands. For the Ancient Egyptians, singing was on the of the main vehicles that took people to the next life. As already noted (p. 87), members of the aboriginal Wägilak clan in Arnhem Land, Australia, intoned the names

of the departed in song as their souls were pulled into the deep
waters of Blue Mud Bay. For them song, known as *manikay*, had
the effect of speeding the passage of the deceased to their ances-
tral home.

A second group of songs and chants related to death and collected in the Hebrides by Carmichael has more theological content.
They are cast in the form of prayers and invocations mouthed by
those concerned about and preparing for their own deaths. The
evangelical Christian doctrine of Christ buying the salvation of
the human soul through the shedding of his blood is prominent
in chants emanating both from the Protestant northern islands of
Lewis, Harris and North Uist and the Catholic southern isles of
South Uist, Vatersay, Barra and Eriskay. So, too, are the themes
of penitence, repentance and forgiveness of sin. In the chants from
the Catholic islands, as one might expect, there is more emphasis
on confession and absolution from a priest and anointing with oil
in the last rite of extreme unction. These themes are prominent
in this hymn, which Carmichael describes as 'one of many which
used to be sung by the Catholics of the Western Isles':

> Thou great God of salvation,
> Pour Thy grace on my soul
> As the sun of the heights
> Pours its love on my body.
>
> I must needs die,
> Nor know I when or where,
> If I die without Thy grace
> I am thus lost everlastingly.
>
> Death of oil and repentance,
> Death of joy and of peace,

> Death of grace and forgiveness,
> Death of Heaven and life with Christ.[16]

Commenting on this hymn, which he entitles 'Happy death', Carmichael writes:

> In the Roman Catholic communities of the west, '*bàs sona*' (happy death) is a phrase frequently heard among the people. When these words are used they imply that the dying person has been confessed and anointed, and that the death-hymn has been intoned over him. Under these conditions the consolation of the living in the loss of the loved one is touching. The old people speak of '*bàs sona*' with exultant satisfaction, and would wish above all things on earth that '*bàs sona*' may be their own portion when the time comes for them to go.[17]

Carmichael notes that in the Roman Catholic islands there is also an acknowledgement of the doctrine of purgatory, the intermediate post-mortem state in which the souls of the departed will be tested and cleansed to make them ready for heaven. He quotes a chant from Barra describing those in purgatory as being 'fanned by the white wings of the fair angels of heaven' so that they become 'whiter than the swan of the songs, the seagull of the waves and the snow of the peaks'.[18] There is, however, no mention of purgatory in any of the death blessings and soul leadings found in the *Carmina Gadelica*. Nor is there any real exposition of the Christian doctrine of resurrection from the dead as expressed in the creeds of the church. There is, as we have seen, an emphasis on the state of sleep that follows death, but virtually nothing on the rising at the last day, as expressed in the well-known prayer 'that the souls of the faithful departed may rest in peace and rise in glory'. Rather there seems more of a sense of souls going straight to heaven, led there by the angels with the *anamchairde*, or mourning women, singing them on their way. There is almost nothing about hell, and very little about God's judgement, although it is hinted at in this chant entitled 'The Day of Death':

> The black wrath of the God of life
> Is upon the soul of gloom as it goes;
> The white wrath of the King of the stars
> Is upon the soul of the dumb concealments.
>
> A perfect calm is on sea and on land,
> Peace is on moor and on meadow,
> The King's joyful glance and smile
> Are to the feeble one down on ocean.
>
> Day of peace and of joy
> The bright day of my death;
> May Michael's hand seek me
> On the white sunny day of my salvation.[19]

In his commentary on this chant, Carmichael writes:

> The old people had a great desire for good weather at the death and burial of a person. It was a good sign that the elements should be at peace at that time. There were two reasons for this. If there was peace on earth it was a sign that there was peace in heaven and a welcome for him who had gone and that the King of all creatures was at peace with him and His own two mighty arms open to take the immortal soul home to Himself. And if there

was peace on earth this gave opportunity to friends and kindred to come to the burial and take farewell of the body in the natural earth and in the grave of the fathers.

If the weather was bad it was a sign that God was wroth. And the bad weather kept friends and kindred from coming to the burial. If the day was wet or misty it was a sign that the King of the elements was pouring wrath on the earth. If the day was black, dark and stormy it showed that God, the Creator of all creatures, was pouring the black wrath of His grief on the soul of him who had gone. If it was a day of snow this was a sign that the white wrath of God was upon the bruised soul that had gone over the black river of death.[20]

There is a third category of death chant or croon mentioned by several of those writing about Highland and Island mourning rituals and funerals in the nineteenth century. This is the keen, or lament, sometimes sung individually by a bereaved relative but more often performed by designated mourning women, either immediately following death in the house of the deceased or as they followed the coffin along the coffin road to the graveyard.

The tradition of keening is found in many cultures. Noel O'Donoghue suggests that it goes back to the ancient Hebrew tradition of lamentation, expressing both individual and communal grief, and notes on the basis of his reading of commentaries on the biblical Book of Lamentations that 'these dirges were of a ritual character and were normally uttered by a professionally trained class of women'.[21] The Wägilak *manikay*, which accompanies all stages of mourning and funerary rituals, has the function of both the death croon and the keen or communal lament. In the words of Samuel Curkpatrick, an ethnomusicologist who has lived with the Wägilak and made a detailed study of their mourning rituals:

'In hearing and performing *manikay*, individuals are woven into a greater *raki* (string) that connects the present with the past and extends into the future, drawing us on into the profound deep – into the essential core. With heterophonic concord, different vocal strands are interwoven in expressive unity. Severance, grief and upheaval are surrounded with vital life, pulling families and individuals together in a living community that is ongoing and not limited by separations of death. Amid the exuberance of life in song, death is transformed.'[22]

Known as *an caoineadh*, the keen has been a particularly important part of Irish folk culture, where it was for long a centrepiece of the traditional wake. Partly prepared and partly extempore, it was delivered in a kind of plaintive recitative, with mourners often echoing or joining in with the emotionally intense wailing of the lead singer, known as the *bean chaointe* or keening woman. The practice was first noted in Ireland by the chronicler Giraldus Cambrensis (Gerald of Wales) in the late 1100s, and survived into the twentieth century. Like the *manikay* of the Wägilak, keening had a dual function, both speeding the passage of the departed soul into the next world and having a cathartic effect on those left behind by expressing and relieving their grieving and allowing them to move on. In the words of Mary Mclaughlin, a singer and teacher who has made a detailed study of the Irish tradition of keening, 'the *bean chaointe* in effect took mourners with her to the very edge of the Otherworld to say farewell to their loved ones . . . One of the functions of the keen is to help the bereaved navigate the liminal stage of the mourning ritual, so they can move from one state to another and adjust to life without their loved one.'[23]

In the Highlands and Islands of Scotland the intoning of the keen (*caoine* in Gaelic) had deep primal roots. The musicologist John Purser has suggested that it may have started as a pre-Christian lament and had its ultimate origin in birdsong. One of the earliest known Gaelic songs, the 'pi-li-li-liu', which seems to have served as a *caoine*, probably derived from the song of the redshank. In Purser's words, 'The mournful call of the redshank is as near to the cry of pi-li-li-liu as you can ask for, the choice of consonants and vowels matching the bird's evocative cry at the edge of the sea, inhabiting the edge of the land on which man lives, and the ocean which represents the eternal life.'[24]

Purser goes on to note that 'the people of Islay used to call one of the seabirds the *caoineteach*, or bird of lament, whose cry heard in the night anticipated a death and also represented the cries of the mourners – in particular the women keening. A bird of death is also heard in Jura.' He provides a fascinating analysis of the structure of the Gaelic keen: 'The *caoine* was in three parts: a deep murmuring repetition of the name of the dead; a dirge (in Gaelic *tuiream*) in which the dead person's character and virtues are evoked; and the third part was the call or cry (in Gaelic *sesig-bhias*) – a chorus using meaningless syllables, perhaps to establish contact with the other world, as may have been the case in fairy songs.'[25]

Keening, almost always undertaken by women, either directly and spontaneously mourning the loss of their own husbands or children, or in their capacity as semi-professional mourning women, continued in the Highlands and Islands well into the nineteenth century. Lord Teignmouth noted in 1836: 'The funeral wail, which contrasted strangely with the succeeding mirth, has fallen into disuse. Yet, so late as in the year 1824, a poor widow woman, in Morvern, followed the remains of her only son to the grave, and sang extemporaneously his lament, to an old plaintive air, enumerating all his virtues, from his own house to the place of interment nearly a mile distant, in beautiful and tender poetry.'[26]

Writing in 1904, Alexander Carmichael gives a full and fascinating account of the role of the *bean-tuirim* or mourning woman in Hebridean funerals, while at the same time providing a further insight into coffin roads, drawn from his own native island of Lismore:

> In Lismore the place over which, whether by design or by accident, a funeral procession travels is ever after considered sacred and as a right of way.
>
> In Barra a corpse is left forty-eight hours above ground, in Uist from three to five nights.
>
> The '*séis*', '*séisig*' or '*séisig-bhàis*', death mourning, or death music, was the mourning in the house after the death. The '*tuiream*' or '*turim*', lament, was the mourning in the open after the journey to the place of burial.
>
> '*Gul, gal*', weeping or sobbing, was applied to professional mourning. This has fallen into disuse in Scotland, though it is still practised in Ireland, where it is called '*caoineadh*', keening. The writer prevailed upon a woman in Barra to give a practical illustration of this lost and almost forgotten art. The burial was that of a crofter fisherman who died young . . .
>
> The '*bean-tuirim*', rehearsing- or lamenting-woman, was tall and handsome, though somewhat gaunt and bony, with long features and long arms. At first she was reluctant to sing, but by degrees she came to use her magnificent voice to the full and the result was striking in the extreme. She and I followed the body as it was carried in simple fashion on three staves by a man at either end of each. The woman rehearsed the grief, the bitter grief, of the winsome young widow, the cries, the bitter cries, of the helpless young children, asking,

plaintively asking, who would now bring them the corn from the breird [the first fruits of the crop], the meal from the mill, the fish from the sea and the birds from the rocks? Who indeed? No one now, since he was laid low. She then rehearsed the sorrows of the poor and the needy, the friendless and the aged whom he had been wont to help. Who would help them now? Who indeed? No one now, since he was laid low.[27]

Carmichael goes on to recount a strange anecdote about the last *bean-tuirim* on the island of Tiree:

In Tiree the '*bean-tuirim*' or mourning woman, was found until the middle of last century. There was some real feeling between the last mourning woman and a neighbour called Domhnall Ruadh, Red Donald. At their last encounter the woman said, 'I will make thee live after thy death, Red Donald'. The man died and the mourning woman took her place at the head of the funeral procession according to custom. Beneath her cloak she carried a cat, and at the end of each verse of her elegy the cat called out. The young were amused, but the older were shocked to see the woman's malice and her misuse of her position, she was never again asked to mourn at a funeral, and the custom finally died out through her unseemly conduct.

The person who told Carmichael this story, an elderly crofter who swore to its veracity, quoted the saying:

A wicked woman will get her prayer,
Though her soul shall not get mercy.[28]

There is more than a hint here that with her wicked curse and her cat, this particular mourning woman had something of the witch about her. In general, however, the *bean-tuirim* seems to have been highly regarded as a valuable and appreciated member of the community, much like the midwife, whose role and function she sometimes seems to have shared and with whom she was often bracketed. Carmichael notes that in Barra there was a midwife and a mourning woman in every township. They were provided by the inhabitants of the township with free summer grass and winter fodder for their animals.

Carmichael describes the activities of several other professional mourning women in the Hebrides. He notes that when one of them accidentally came across the funeral procession of a woman being taken from Benbecula for burial at Rodal on Harris, 'she instinctively joined in the weeping and wailing'. Quoting a death lament from Barra at the end of the eighteenth century, sung during the funeral procession of a well-loved man who had been particularly kind to an orphaned family, he writes: 'The "*bean-tuiream*" followed the body, every now and then striking the coffin with her hands like a drum, and making all the din possible, and keeping time with the movements of the men. All the virtues of the dead, and a few more, were mentioned and extolled, and the genealogy for many generations praised and lauded.'[29]

The effect of the moaning of the mourning women must have been enhanced by the sound of the waves breaking on the seashore which so often accompanied Hebridean burials. Carmichael describes the very first hymn that appears in the *Carmina Gadelica* being intoned by old people 'in low tremulous unmeasured cadences like the moving and moaning, the soughing and the sighing, of the ever-murmuring sea on their own wild shores'. He continues: 'I have known men and women of eighty, ninety, and a hundred years of age continue the practice of their lives in going from one to two miles to the seashore to join their voices with the voicing of the waves.'[30] We are brought back here to the idea of the sea, and especially the western ocean, as the ultimate abode of the dead, their souls carried down to it from the streams that run past Highland and Hebridean graveyards. We are brought back, too, to the words of George Matheson, the blind minister, as he stood in the front room of his manse in Innellan, hearing the sounds of the Clyde, reflecting 'heaven begins here, and immortality', and writing his great hymn:

> O Love that wilt not let me go,
> I rest my weary soul in thee;
> I give thee back the life I owe,
> that in thine ocean depths its flow
> may richer, fuller be.

All this has taken us some way from where we started at the Piper's Cairn on the coffin road on Eigg. Yet we can come back to piping because it, too, provided an evocative and melancholy soundtrack for Hebridean funerals, its plaintive sound merging with the keening of the mourning women and the moaning of the sea. In his notes on the *bean-tuirim* Carmichael comments on the key role that pipers played in funerals. He singled out John MacDonald, who played at many funerals on North Uist until his death in the early 1880s. Carmichael also writes movingly about the practice found on several islands of singing the familiar death croon about going home to eternal sleep to the accompaniment of a well-known pipe tune associated with a secular song, 'Bonnet and feather and tartan and plaid': 'The tune was played at funerals in Lewis, Harris and Skye down to Disruption times. I spoke to people who had heard it played at a funeral at Aoidh in Lewis. They said that the scene and the tune were singularly impressive – the moaning of the sea, the mourning of the women, and the lament of the pipes over all as the body was carried to its home of winter, to its home of autumn, of spring and of summer; never could they forget the solemnity of the occasion, where all was so natural and so beautiful, and nature seemed to join in the feelings of humanity.'[31]

Along with Kenneth Macleod, Alexander Carmichael has dominated this chapter and rightly so, because he is the most illuminating and authoritative commentator on the chants and songs associated with dying and funerals in the Hebrides and the Highlands. He himself died in Edinburgh on 6 June 1912. Four days later, his coffin, draped with a tartan plaid, was conveyed to Oban by train and thence to Lismore by the MacBrayne's steamer *Fingal*. Islanders carried it on their shoulders from the pier to the island graveyard where, in the words of the *Oban Times* reporter, a Gaelic psalm was 'sung to the plaintive notes of "Coleshill" by male voices in the Highland style in the peaceful churchyard girded by the loch and its enclosing mountains'.[32] His headstone was engraved with a Celtic cross with interlacing spirals and an inscription in Gaelic which, translated into English, reads: 'Be my soul in peace with thee, Brightness of the mountains. Valiant Michael, meet thou my soul.'

Let us give Kenneth Macleod the last word, taking us back to Eigg and anticipating the supernatural phenomena which are the subject of the next chapter. For him, the island of his birth 'was alive with legends and other-world beings. Mysterious tales made the caves and the kirkyard a terror by night; the water-sprite washed in a certain burn the shrouds of the dying; and on the first Monday of each quarter, a fire-ship passed the island at midnight, with a long lean black creature on board, a fiddle in his hand, and he ever playing, and dancing, and laughing, while 'tween-decks lost souls clanked their chains, and shrieked, and cursed.'[33]

7

Premonitions and Apparitions
Kintail

The 26-mile Kintail coffin road from Glen Strathfarrar to the graveyard at Clachan Duich on the north shore of Loch Duich is one of the longest coffin roads in the Highlands and features on several websites as a long-distance walk. There are a number of interesting accounts of happenings along it, including one that takes us into the realm of the paranormal.

Before recounting this ghostly tale and introducing the theme of the second sight which is the main subject of this chapter, it is worth quoting two vivid stories about journeys along the Kintail coffin road in the late nineteenth century. The first, recounted by Peter Macdonald, the head keeper on the Broulin estate, indicates how matter-of-fact the business of carrying a body along a coffin road could be and mingles respect for the dead with natural curiosity. Macdonald told Archibald Robertson how he had walked from Glen Strathfarrar to the graveyard adjoining the ruined church of St Dubthac's at Clachan Duich with the body of the baby son of a fellow keeper: 'We came to cross the river above the Falls of Glomach. I had never seen the falls before. I had the coffin under my arm, but I thought the wee fellow wouldn't mind, and so I dropped down the hillside for a few hundred feet to where I could see the falls and "we" had a good look and then went on our way to Kintail.'[1] Another story originally recounted by a neighbouring keeper, Kenneth McLellan, recalled the funeral of Mrs MacRae, 'a big heavy woman', whose body had to be transported from Pait on the south-east shore of Loch Monar to Kintail Church, a journey of more than 20 miles over rough, mountainous terrain. A relief party of bearers from Kintail took over at Carnach. Iain Thomson, who wrote about his experiences working as a shepherd in the area of Loch Morar in the late 1950s in his book *Isolation Shepherd*, gives a vivid account of Mrs MacRae's final journey as it was told to him by a local stalker, Kenny MacKay:

> With fitting deference to the solemn occasion, the procession wound its way through Pait, west along the Gead Loch side and into Corrie Each. The cortege bore on gravely and with dignity. Some were employed as coffin bearers, others, more importantly on such an arduous trek, to convey the victuals, contained mostly in large wooden kegs. The day grew warm. Certain ungracious comment regarding the deceased lady's weight filtered through the ranks of the sweating bearers. At each coffin resting point along the path, stones were added to an existing cairn, or a fresh cairn was piously raised. The warmth grew oppressive. The procession grew thirsty. By and by the frequency of the stops precluded dignified cairn building obsequies. Before the final steep climb out of Corrie Each the Kintail men, waiting high above on the march to join the oncoming mourners, observed below them formality dispensed to the point where brow mopping bearers seated on the coffin were libaciously quaffing unwise amounts of the otherwise ample supplies. One might consider it befitting that

Mrs MacRae, to quote common parlance, was enthusi-
astically afforded 'a good send off'.[2]

Something rather more spooky happened along the route of
the Kintail coffin road when the English mountaineer and bot-
anist Frank Smythe was on a day walk in the Highlands in the
mid 1930s. In his book *The Mountain Vision*, published in 1941,
he gave this account of what he described as his 'strangest experience' in a lifetime of climbing and long-distance walking:

> I was walking over the hills from Morvich on Loch
> Duich to Glen Glomach and the Falls of Glomach. It
> was a bright sunny day, and there was nothing in the
> least sinister about the vista of cloud-chequered hills and
> the distant blue of the sea. In crossing the ridge before
> dropping down to Glen Glomach I passed for a short
> distance through a grassy defile. There was nothing out-
> wardly sinister about this pass and the sun shone warmly
> into it, yet when I entered it I at once encountered —
> that is the only word to express it — an atmosphere
> of evil. Something terrible had once happened at that
> spot, and time had failed to dissipate the atmosphere
> created by it. I was interested in my reaction to the
> place, and as it was as good as any for lunch decided to
> halt there and see whether I could make anything of it.
> Ghosts and ham sandwiches are scarcely companions,
> but after lunch, when my pipe was well alight, I surren-
> dered myself to contemplation of my environment. As I
> reclined, drowsily smoking, the atmosphere of the defile
> seemed to press upon me with an even greater force
> than before. I did my best to keep my mind unoccu-
> pied with anything, to make myself receptive and allow

imagination a free rein, and this is what I saw, or, as the
sceptical reader will say with perfect justification, what
I imagined I saw.

A score or more of ragged people, men, women
and children, were straggling through the defile. They
appeared very weary, as though they had come a long
way. The pitiful procession was in the midst of the
defile when of a sudden from either side concealed men
leapt to their feet and, brandishing spears, axes and
clubs, rushed down with wild yells on the unfortunates
beneath. There was a short fierce struggle, then a horrible massacre. Not one man, woman or child was left
alive; the defile was choked with corpses.

I got out of the place as quickly as I could. Screams
seemed to din in my ears as I hastened down the broad
heather slopes into Glen Glomach. I am not a superstitious person, but it seemed to me that I was vouchsafed
a backward glimpse into a blood-stained page of
Highland history.[3]

It was only later that Smythe discovered that he had been
walking on the Kintail coffin road. According to a letter that he
wrote to *The Scotsman* after his book was reviewed, he also learned
that massacres of Highlanders by British Government forces had
taken place on the road between Morvich and Glen Glomach in
the aftermath of both the 1715 and 1745 rebellions. I have found no
definite evidence for these but there was certainly a bloody battle
in nearby Glen Shiel during the brief Jacobite rising of 1719 when
British Government forces defeated Highlanders led by Cameron
of Lochiel and Rob Roy Macgregor. The English novelist Colin
Wilson, who developed a strong interest in the paranormal, was
fascinated by Smythe's 'vision', which he described in his own

book *Beyond the Occult* as a psychic experience involving a 'tape recording of a past event somehow imprinted on the scenery'.

Frank Smythe's vivid and disturbing 'flashback' is just one of many well-documented psychic experiences involving Highland and Island coffin roads. Some, like his, take the form of encounters with ghosts and spectres from the past but the majority are premonitions or omens of death, known in Gaelic as *manadhean air bàs*, often in the form of phantom funeral processions which foreshadow and precede real ones. We are here firmly in the realm of the second sight (*dà-shealladh* in Gaelic, literally the two sights), that much discussed feature of the Highland and Hebridean psyche which has played a key role in shaping attitudes to death and dying.

One of the earliest descriptions of manifestations of the second sight in the West Highlands comes from the pen of the Welsh antiquary and Celtic scholar, Edward Lhuyd, during a visit to Argyll in 1699: 'Men with the second sight see a man with a light like the light of the glow-worm, or with fish [scales] over his hair and his clothes, if he is to be drowned; bloody, if he is to be wounded; in his shroud if he is to die in his bed.'[4] What is significant about this description is that the second sight is almost invariably associated with premonitions and omens of death and very rarely with visions of happy events in the future. For this reason, those gifted with the second sight, who were known as seers (*taibhsearan* in Gaelic) were usually very unhappy about possessing it and quite often sought to rid themselves of it through engaging in various rituals.

The fullest early treatment of the subject of Highland second sight comes from Martin Martin, himself a native of Skye, and is based on his travels through the Western Isles in the 1680s and 1690s. He provides one of the most succinct definitions of the phenomenon: 'The second-sight is a singular faculty of seeing an

otherwise invisible object, without any previous means used by
the person that sees it for that end; the vision makes such a lively
impression upon the seers, that they neither see nor think of
anything else, except the vision, as long as it continues.'[5] Martin
goes on to give more than 50 examples, mostly drawn from Skye,
of seers' premonitions of unexpected deaths, which have subsequently come to pass exactly as they saw them, and to list some
of the signals that death was imminent. These included seeing
a chair empty when someone was sitting in it, seeing someone
dressed in a shroud and seeing a spark of fire fall on an arm or
breast, 'a forerunner of a dead child to be seen in the arms of
those persons'. Sudden screams and cries were also common har-
bingers of death.

Among the many detailed accounts that Martin gives of seers'
premonitions that came to pass are three from Skye which involve
funeral processions along coffin roads. The first involves horses,
whom Martin notes could, like children and cows, be gifted with
the second sight.

A horse fastened by the common road on the side of
Loch Skeriness in Skye did break his rope at noonday,
and run up and down without the least visible cause.
About two of the neighbourhood that happened to be at
a little distance and in view of the horse did at the same
time see a considerable number of men about a corpse
directing their course to the church of Snizort; And this
was accomplished within a few days after by the death
of a gentlewoman who lived thirteen miles from that
church and came from another parish from whence very
few came to Snizort to be buried.

One that lived in St Mary's, on the west side of the
isle of Skye, told Mr MacPherson, the minister, and

others, that he saw a vision of a corpse coming towards the church, not by the common road, but by a more rugged way, which rendered the thing incredible, and occasioned his neighbours to call him a fool; but he made them have patience and they would see the truth of what he asserted in a short time: and it fell out accordingly, for one of the neighbourhood died, and his corpse was carried along the same unaccustomed way, the common road being at that time filled with a deep snow. This account was given me by the minister and others living there.

John Macnormand and Daniel MacEwin, travelling along the road, two miles to the north of Snizort Church, saw a body of men coming from the north, as if they had a corpse with them to be buried in Snizort; this determined them to advance towards the river, which was then a little before them, and having waited at the ford, thinking to meet those that they expected with the funeral, were altogether disappointed, for after taking a view of the ground all round them, they discovered that it was only a vision. This was very surprising to them both, for they never saw anything by way of the second-sight before or after that time. This they told their neighbours when they came home, and it happened that about two or three weeks after a corpse came along that road from another parish, from which few or none are brought to Snizort, except persons of distinction, so that this vision was exactly accomplished.[6]

What is interesting in the second of these accounts is that the local parish minister was made aware of the seer's vision and does not seem to have condemned or discounted it. A good number of

Martin's stories indeed suggest endorsement of the second sight by ministers. He himself was at pains to counter scepticism about the phenomenon and the ridiculing of seers by pointing out that they were almost invariably sober, temperate and well-balanced individuals, not given to drink or displaying any signs of insanity. 'The seers are generally illiterate and well meaning people,' he wrote, 'and altogether void of design, nor could I ever learn that any of them made the least gain by it.' He also noted that 'every vision that is seen comes exactly to pass according to the true rules of observation'.[7]

Those writing about Highland and Hebridean customs and folklore in the nineteenth century continued to be struck, like Martin, by the prevalence of the second sight and premonitions and omens of death. Norman MacLeod noted in his 1871 *Reminiscences of a Highland Parish*: 'It is still a very common belief among the peasantry that shadowy funeral processions precede the real ones, and that "warnings" are given of a coming death by the crowing of cocks, the ticking of the death watch, the howling of dogs, voices heard by night, the sudden appearance of undefined forms of human beings passing to and fro, &c.'[8]

Two extremely interesting and extensive collections of stories about ghostly apparitions and premonitions of death in the Hebrides and Highlands were made in the latter half of the nineteenth century, one by a Church of Scotland minister and the other by a Roman Catholic priest. The first was compiled by the great folklorist John Gregorson Campbell, who was born at Kingairloch on the east side of the Morvern peninsula in 1834 and was parish minister on the islands of Coll and Tiree from 1861 until his death in 1891. Based on extensive fieldwork in the period between 1850 and 1880 and on accounts that he obtained directly from those involved, the results of his research were published posthumously in 1902 in a book entitled *Witchcraft & Second*

Sight in the Highlands. It includes substantial separate chapters on Death Warnings and on Second Sight. The former points out that certain families and septs had death warnings peculiar to themselves. Before the death of a member of the Breadalbane family, a bull was heard at night roaring up the hillside. The MacLachlan clan were warned of death by a little bird and a sept of the Macgregors by a whistle. Other signals included shouting, screaming and weeping. In Campbell's words, 'when any of them foreboded death, it was heard where no human being could be, and there was an unearthly tone about it that struck a chill into a hearer's heart'.[9] Particularly frightening was the spectre of a headless horseman that appeared before the death of one of the MacLaines of Lochbuie on Mull.

Campbell's chapter on second sight is particularly detailed. He describes it as an unwanted gift associated especially with Hebrideans and Highlanders, a condition of being 'spectre-haunted' which manifests itself either in sightings of ghosts of the dead revisiting the earth (*tannas*) or apparitions or doubles of living persons (*tamhasg*). Very precise conclusions could be drawn from the circumstances of these latter visions which were nearly always a premonition of death. The nature of the person's clothing indicated how close death was, as did the time that the vision was seen – the later in the day, the more imminent was death.

Many of the premonitions of death experienced by those with second sight took place on public or coffin roads. *Taibhsearan* would regularly see spectral funeral processions and would pull those walking with them to one side to allow the funeral to pass. Otherwise they might find themselves being knocked over or feeling the whole weight of the coffin pressing down on them. Those experiencing such apparitions in Moidart described having one of the staves bearing the coffin thrust into their hands and being compelled to take part in the procession until relieved in due time. It is hardly surprising that there was a widespread reluctance throughout the West Highlands and Hebrides to walk in the middle of a road at night for fear of meeting one of these phantom funeral processions. Campbell noted:

> The doctrine is that the whole ceremony connected with a funeral is gone through in rehearsal by spectres which are the shades, phantoms, appearances, doubles, swarths – or whatever else we choose to call them – of living men, not merely by the shade of the person who is to die, but by the shades of all who are to be concerned in the ceremony. The phantoms go for the wood that is to make the coffin, the nails, the dead-clothes, and whatever else may be required on the occasion; the sounds of the coffin being made are heard, of presses being opened, of glasses rattling; and the melancholy procession has been met in the dead of night wending its way to the churchyard.[10]

Illustrating this point, he mentioned a joiner in Kinloch Rannoch, gifted with the second sight, who emigrated to Australia around 1850 and gave as the chief reason for leaving his native land the frequency with which he saw or heard people coming beforehand for coffins. 'The tools of his trade, plane, hammers, saw, etc., were heard by him at work as distinctly as though he himself were working, and the frequency of the omen preyed so much on his mind that he left the country in the hope of relief. The shades were not those of the people whose death was imminent, but those of their friends and acquaintances, who afterwards proved actually to be the parties who came for the coffin.'[11] There were many similar stories of people being disturbed by mysterious hammering from joiners' workshops in the middle of the night.

Other stories that Campbell collected from those who claimed to have seen phantom funeral processions included one from a man in Tiree who saw a funeral procession leaving a certain house with persons whom he could name acting as coffin bearers. This was at Beltane, the first day of summer. The following Christmas, a death occurred at that house and the funeral took place exactly as he had seen it. A woman living near Loch Scavaig on Skye saw a funeral procession with three coffins passing along a hillside where there was no road. After her death, and two years after her vision, a boat was lost in the loch. The bodies of the three men who had gone down with it were initially buried near a shepherd's hut at the lochside. They were subsequently dug up and carried along the route that the woman had seen in her vision in order to be buried in the local graveyard. A man in Skye encountered a spectral funeral procession at night and walked with it to the churchyard at Portree. He asked whose funeral it was, to be told 'your own'.

A common trope in the stories recounted by John Gregorson Campbell was of encounters with figures appearing with dripping wet clothes and water in their shoes or boots, foreshadowing death by drowning. There were also stories of ghostly figures seen in fishing boats at a time when they were unmanned – as a result such boats were usually shunned and no one would go to sea in them.

Screaming and shouting were often heard before a death. Among the many examples of this mentioned by Campbell was the horrible screaming and shouting heard one summer evening around 1870 in Kingairloch from across Loch Corrie: 'In a line with the shouting lay a ship at anchor and the burying-ground on the other side of the loch. The cry was like that of a goat or buck being killed, a bleating which bears a horrible resemblance to the human voice. Next night the master of the ship was drowned, no one knew how. The man on the watch said that when sitting in the stern of the ship he saw the skipper go below, and then clanking as if the chain were being paid out. He heard and saw nothing further. The night was fine.'[12]

It was regarded as a good omen if a light was seen before a person's death. The *dreag* was a light seen in the sky, leaving a tail (*dreallsach*) behind it. Sometimes it stopped above the house where the death was to occur, at other times it proceeded from the house to the churchyard along the line the funeral was to take, usually along the coffin road if there was one. These lights were sometimes known as 'corpse candles'. Campbell also mentions greenish bright lights seen moving from place to place in a darkened room shortly before a death took place. These were said to be spirits awaiting the soul of the dying person. When the body lay stretched out, these lights were seen hovering near 'and perhaps seven or eight butterflies fluttered through the room. They moved about the chest in which were the bannocks to be used at the funeral, or the winding sheet, and about the cupboard in which the glasses were.'[13] He did not record whether these were the yellow butterflies mentioned by Carmichael (pp. 103–4).

Campbell also collected several stories about the return of the dead. It was said of a sept of the MacDonalds on Tiree that when one died and the body was laid out for the wake, all the dead of the race entered the room, went round the body, upon which each lay his hand, and then in solemn procession marched out again. This was said to happen at every death of a member of the sept, but only those who had the second sight could see the shades. The spirits of the dead came back to reveal secrets and give good advice. Notoriously bad men, misers and oppressors of the poor were believed after death to wander about their former haunts. Old women on Tiree placed springs of *mòthan* (trailing pearlwort) above their front doors to prevent the spirits of the dead from entering the house. It was also customary to place a drink of water beside the corpse in case the dead should return. In his earlier travels around the Highlands and Islands in the late 1830s Lord Teignmouth had come across another way of chasing spirits away: 'The illumination of the house immediately after the decease and the late wake, may be doubtless partly attributed to the superstitious notion of chasing evil spirits from the corpse.'[14]

Emphasising the special reverence felt for graves and burial places in the Highlands and Hebrides, Campbell noted the continuing strong belief that the last person to be buried had to watch over the graveyard until the next funeral. What is perhaps particularly significant about his extensive collection of supernatural and paranormal occurrences is that they virtually all come from predominantly Protestant communities. As one would expect, the Roman Catholic islands of the southern Outer Hebrides yielded an equally rich crop of similar stories. The most extensive collection of them was made in the late 1880s and early 1890s by Father Allan McDonald, Roman Catholic priest on South Uist and Eriskay from 1884 to 1894 and on Eriskay on its own from 1894 until his death in 1905.

The material which Father McDonald collected, predominantly on South Uist and Eriskay, was an important source for an enquiry into the phenomenon of second sight in the Scottish Highlands and Islands undertaken by the Society for Psychical Research in 1894 and 1895 and funded by the Third Marquess of Bute. One of those most involved in this enquiry was Peter Dewar, parish minister of North Bute, who was by no means the only Church of Scotland minister in this period to be very interested in psychical research and open to second sight and other manifestations of extrasensory perception. Dewar developed a close

friendship with Father McDonald and collaborated with him on
research in this area. This is how he described his own findings
based on interviews with 'several of the noted Eriskay Seers':

> The cases one meets within Eriskay are cases of lights
> of a super normal character – foreshadowing deaths;
> phantasmal funeral processions seen in many instances
> months before the deaths they seemed to presage; pro-
> cessions of the dead by which the Seers sometimes are
> met and carried in an unconscious state, for considerable
> distances; phantasmal writings or the hum of phan-
> tasmal voices engaged in conversation heard some days
> or even weeks before a death; chests containing grave
> clothes (kept by the people in view of any emergency
> that might occur) being seen to open and shut with a
> loud noise a few days before neighbours called to beg
> the loan of a winding sheet or shroud; phantom ships
> seen by fishermen on a certain part of the coast where
> subsequently vessels of an exactly similar description
> were wrecked and the lives of the crew lost.[15]

An extremely detailed account of the 1894–5 enquiry by
the Society for Psychical Research was written by John Lorne
Campbell and Trevor Hall and published in 1968 under the title
Strange Things. This was also the title that Father McDonald gave
to one of the collections of stories, reports and anecdotes that
he assembled in a series of notebooks which he made available
to the enquiry. The contents of such of these notebooks as sur-
vive are published in this book and make extremely interesting
reading. Many of them recount very similar apparitions, omens
and premonitions of death to those noted a few decades earlier
by John Gregorson Campbell. There are numerous accounts of

the appearance of strange lights presaging death, the cries of the drowning being heard and people seeing coffins being carried along roads and standing aside to avoid them. There is a story from South Uist of a corpse which had been laid out on a plank in a house rising from the dead and another about a carpenter who twice saw a lamb surrounded by rays of light standing in a coffin that he was making. In Eriskay in the spring of 1887 a bird with a terrible scream was heard flitting across the island from time to time at night. In the autumn of that year a number of young people on the island died from measles, including the daughter of a man who had heard the bird pushing against the door of his house and making 'as much noise as a man would'.

The 'strange things' which feature in McDonald's notebooks include two accounts of phantom funeral processions, the first of which is notable for its mention of bagpipes:

> A Mrs Morrach Campbell was coming along with Oighrig then about 11 years old from Northbay, Barra, to Eoligarry, when they reached the Tràigh Mhór or Great Strand. Both heard the pipes playing behind them. Both of them were afraid. The piping continued the whole way till they reached Eoligarry. They both thought it the warning of a funeral at which the pipes would be played coming to Kilbarra graveyard in front of Eoligarry house.
>
> Mrs MacCormick says that her sister Mary MacMillan, still alive in Eriskay, when at service in Kilbride farm South Uist at night-fall at the Cnoc-a-dea saw a phantom funeral, and that she went aside out of the way, and that she heard the creak of the coffin passing. She thinks that Mary recognised the people attending the funeral.[16]

Two further premonitions involving bagpipes were recorded by McDonald in February 1896:

> Neil Johnston, Haun, Eriskay, aged about 60, says that when he was a little boy he saw a trunk in the house open and heard bagpipes that were in the trunk give a groan as bagpipes give when being blown up. His mother said that it would not be long before the pipes would be taken out for a funeral. As far as he can remember they were taken out for the funeral of a grand-aunt of his called Catherine.
>
> Neil Johnston also says that he heard that Alex MacDonald, piper, Kilphedir, still alive in 1895, had prepared a sheepskin as a bag for his pipes and had laid it aside on the top of a bed, and that his wife one day heard this skin give a groan and asked her husband if he had been putting wind into it and that he said that he had not. Not long after the skin in question had to be got ready for the funeral of a brother of the piper called Malcolm, belonging to North Lochboisdale, who shot himself accidentally while hunting ducks.[17]

Visions and apparitions of future funerals continued to occur in the southern Hebrides well into the twentieth century. The well-known Barra storyteller John MacPherson, known as the Coddy, related how during the First World War a sailor from South Uist came home and visited his neighbour, MacAskill, who then walked part of the way back late at night with his guest. Suddenly the sailor told MacAskill to stop and stand at the side of the road as there was a funeral coming. The two men duly did so and after a few minutes, the sailor said, 'now you can come to the middle of the road – the funeral has passed. Before I come

back, such and such a man will be dead.' By the time the sailor
next came back on leave, the man whose name he had mentioned
had indeed died. When MacCaskill asked him how he had been
able to predict this, the sailor replied, 'My prediction is always
true. I guessed it was going to be that man by the appearance of
the mourners I saw following the funeral.'[18]

A story told to the Coddy by a hotel keeper in Polacharra,
South Uist, is one of several in which objects used at funeral
wakes, such as beer casks, are seen jumping around: 'Any time
that there is a funeral to be in the district, on the socket on which
I put the beer cask I can see it sometimes jumping and hear it
thumping pretty often. It is customary to have drinks at funerals
in Uist, and every time there is a funeral I can hear this noise a
few days before. And as soon as the funeral party comes to collect
the beer and clear away, I don't hear the *manadh* any more, until
there is another funeral. In fact, I heard several times the cart that
was going to carry the jar away coming to the house.'[19]

The existence of the second sight, and its particular associa-
tion with forebodings and warnings of death, is not peculiar to
the Scottish Highlands and Islands. Martin Martin noted that it
was known in Wales, the Isle of Man and even Holland. Most
folklorists and anthropologists are, however, agreed in seeing it
as being a particular and distinctive characteristic of Highland
and Hebridean belief and culture which is often traced back to
ancient Celtic roots. With his prophecies, Columba is sometimes
seen as the first seer or *taibhsear* to be gifted with the second
sight. John Gregorson Campbell believed that second sight was a
distinctively Celtic characteristic, and noted: 'The suggestion that
it is the remains of the magic of the druids is not unreasonable. In
every age there are individuals who are spectre-haunted, and it is
probable enough that the sage Celtic priests, assuming the spectres to be external, reduced the gift of seeing them to a system,

a belief in which formed part of their teaching. This accounts for the circumstance that the second sight has flourished more among the Celts than any other race.'[20]

Writing about *The Folklore of the Scottish Highlands* in 1976, Anne Ross basically concurs with this view. Having given several examples of the exercise of the 'Sight', as she calls it, to predict and foretell death, she observes: 'This preoccupation with death and all its trappings is very typical of the Celts and goes right back to the ancient widespread cult of the dead and the worship of graves and the ancestors. It is also very much a reflection of the Celtic passion for the tabulation of everything, and listing all things in a fit manner; nothing was left to happen as it would; everything must be explicable and predictable. This again is a very archaic trait in the whole Celtic character.'[21]

Dr Lorn Macintyre, an author who has made a special study of second sight, believes that its particular prevalence in the Highlands and the Hebrides is partly explained by the isolation of so many of its inhabitants: 'Think of a widow sitting on her own staring into a peat fire for hours. Perhaps the glow hypnotised her into some kind of trance and created a vision. These people who had second sight lived between two worlds.' He also points to the longevity of the tradition, which may well have its origin in pagan times, and the number of Gaelic terms that describe aspects of it. 'Second sight is known to descend through families, as in my own to the present,' he points out, 'and it is involuntary, visited on people, none of whom want it because it so often presages death. In that respect, second sight is totally different from spiritualism, where the dead are apparently contacted through seances, mediums and Ouija boards, warning of tragedies to come.' While conceding that premonitions of impending death are 'very frightening and debilitating to those with second sight, like my late aunt, both of whose parents had it,' he points out that in the devout, fear was succeeded 'by acceptance of the biblical maxim that inevitably in the midst of life we are in death', and that their visions were 'part of the interwoven fabric of life and death. Even the spectres and ghosts which haunted certain Highland houses were not seen as particularly unsettling but rather as longstanding and relatively natural and benign phenomena which linked the living with the dead, like the family portraits on the walls.'[22]

Whatever its origins and explanation, the pervasive culture of omens and signs foreshadowing death led the inhabitants of the Highlands and the Hebrides to make detailed preparations for their own funerals long before they happened. Lord Teignmouth was struck by the particular customs associated with this advance planning, 'one of which is that of the bride considering it to be one of her first duties after marriage, to prepare her winding-sheet for her interment: another, which was formerly very common, that of the woman preparing as much of the tartan of her own or her husband's clan, as served for a mort-cloth for her coffin or that of her husband.'[23] In similar vein Norman MacLeod noted:

It has been the custom of the poorest persons to have all their dead clothes prepared for years before their death, so as to insure a decent orderly interment. To make these clothes was a task often imposed upon the ladies, or females in a parish who were good at their needle. The pattern of the shroud was a fixed one, and special instructions were given regarding it by the initiated. Such things are common even now among Highland families who have emigrated to Glasgow. A short time ago a highly respectable lady in that city, when she found that her illness was dangerous, gave a confidential servant the key of a box, where, in the event of death, all would be found that was required to dress her body for the grave. The old wrapping of the body was woollen cloth, and the Gaelic term used to express it, *ollanachd*, which may be translated 'woollening', is still used to describe the dressing of the body before burial.[24]

MacLeod went on to make a further interesting observation about the way in which bodies were traditionally covered before burial: 'The Gaelic term still in use for a coffin (*caisil chrò*), the "wattle enclosure," points to what we doubt not was peculiar to the Highlands, that of surrounding the dead body with slender branches of trees, and bending them firmly together with *withs* or twisted rods of hazel or willow, and thus interring it.'[25] This practice was also mentioned by Thomas Ratcliffe Barnett, who noted that in early times before coffins were widely available, 'the corpse was enclosed in a case of wickerwork, or long saplings placed side by side, and bound with green withies. These green withies, when twisted together, acted as carrying ropes.'[26] He comments that this practice was universal in 'the ancient Celtic church'. The modern trend for 'eco-friendly' natural burials using biodegradable coffins marks a welcome return to this ancient Celtic tradition.

8

Wakes and Whisky

Barra

The coffin road on Barra, known as Beul a'Bhealaich, cuts across the middle of the island, starting just north of Earsary on the east coast. It was used for transporting the bodies of those who had lived and died on the rocky eastern side of the island to St Brendan's Church at Craigston, the oldest church on Barra and the only Catholic church on the island until the building of Our Lady Star of the Sea in Castlebay in 1888 and St Barr's in Northbay in 1906. The graveyard at the end of the coffin road lies beyond St Brendan's Church on Barra's west coast. Among those buried there is Father John MacMillan, who was born in Barra in 1880 and served as a priest on Eigg, Benbecula and at Ballachulish before eventually returning to his native shores. He was the model for Father John Macalister, the priest in Compton Mackenzie's novel *Whisky Galore*. Around 1,200 mourners attended his funeral in 1951 with six pipers leading the procession, which made its way from the townships of Craigston and Borve to St Brendan's graveyard.

Beul a'Bhealaich is the most westerly of all the Hebridean coffin roads, and so the one nearest to the mythical Tír na nÓg, a point not lost on Thomas Ratcliffe Barnett, who waxed lyrical about it in his book, *The Road to Rannoch and the Summer Isles*, published in 1924 and dedicated to Kenneth Macleod:

The children of tempest long to return from many a
weary wandering on the rim of the world to their little
thatch huts on these desolate isles . . . I have seen them
bringing back their dead across the stormy Minch to
Barra Bay and in past Castle Kishmul in the sunset. A
cart full of clean-smelling meadow hay and a group of
grave-faced friends are waiting. Then a solemn rumbling
of wheels as the little company follow their dead over
the old road to the west side. There, in the darkening
by the white sands, a sound of keening comes from a
cottage door . . . There are still men of the mystic soul
who search out here, at the back of the world, for the
Isle of Lost Youth.[1]

Barra is among the most Catholic of all the Hebridean islands.
In the 2011 census, 81.5 per cent of its islanders identified as
Roman Catholic; only in South Uist was there a higher proportion (90 per cent). Largely for that reason, it has retained longer
than anywhere else many of the distinctive Hebridean traditions
associated with death and dying. We are fortunate to have two
very full and illuminating accounts of the beliefs and practices
surrounding death on Barra in the middle of the twentieth
century. Both show the persistence of rites and customs which
had largely disappeared by this time in much of the rest of the
Hebrides and the Highlands.

The first account comes in a book entitled *Reflections of the Isle
of Barra*, first published in 1942 by the Catholic Book Club and
written by Donald Buchanan, a native of the island who trained
as a doctor in Edinburgh and practised for most of his career
in London. He returned annually to Barra and published this
book just a year before his death. By far the longest chapter is
on the religion of Barra. Buchanan, a devout Catholic, was keen

to refute the notion that the islanders harboured any lingering pagan Celtic superstitions about death. Interestingly, he makes no reference at all to the second sight but he does explicitly say that he has never heard anything 'which might suggest belief in the transmigration of souls, whether or not this was a belief of the Druids, who were a late product of the pagan world'. This explicit distancing of the islanders' beliefs about what follows death from any taint of Buddhist or Hindu notions of reincarnation, and indeed from the Zoroastrian idea of the soul's gradual departure from the body, as discussed on p. 100, is accompanied by the robust assertion that 'there is really nothing in the religious beliefs of our time that can be attributed to pagan impurity'.[2] Rather, he is at pains to demonstrate the islanders' adherence to orthodox Christian doctrine and the teaching of the Church.

In describing the islanders' approach to death, Buchanan begins by paying tribute to the considerable role played by the voluntary attentions of friends and neighbours in caring for the sick and dying: 'In the period penultimate to death, charitable visitation is much in evidence; even after death the spirit of charity endures, and friends and neighbours volunteer for whatever labours are inseparable from the obsequies. There is no undertaker, no mortuary and no hearse in Barra, and I expect this form of modernisation will be about the last to arrive and I hope it will be deferred until life deserts Barra in response to the final siren.'[3]

He then goes on to describe what happens after a death:

> Certain women who are recognised for the 'vocation' visit the house, lay out the body and robe it in a shroud made and decorated by themselves out of plain glazed white linen. The body is laid out on a table, with the ritual and symbols associated with death, while the local

carpenter makes the coffin out of plain deal, which until recently he cut out of large planks usually obtained as jetsam on the shore, by means of a species of cross saw worked perpendicularly by two operators.

Relays of people visit the premises of the dead and offer up their prayers of intercession. The watch and prayers continue through the night, with intervals of story-telling, which may sound profane but fits the occasion quite inoffensively. This continues for the period the body remains unburied, which usually extends over two nights, a shorter period than is generally allowed in more popular centres. In recent years it has become a custom to convey the body to the church overnight or on the funeral morning when a Requiem Mass is celebrated.

On the day of the burial all the men of the neighbourhood gather at the church or home to convey the remains to the cemetery. The coffin is placed on a bier arranged like a six-handled stretcher with the handles arranged in transverse fashion. The men march in pairs and the coffin is carried by six men, three on each side. The carriers are relieved at frequent intervals upon the commands of a marshal. Friends who are familiar with the family burying ground have the grave prepared upon the arrival of the funeral procession. There is a short religious service at the graveside, and after the interment the assembly finally goes on its knees for a parting intercession.[4]

Many of these elements are familiar from accounts of practices in the nineteenth century quoted earlier in this book: the laying-out of the body; the role of the designated mourning women (though there is no mention of chanting the death croon or keening); the two-night vigil over the body in the house; the digging of the grave by friends; and the carrying of the coffin to the cemetery.

A more detailed and academic examination of attitudes and practices relating to death on Barra is to be found in a London University doctoral thesis undertaken in 1954 by Frank Vallee, a Canadian social anthropologist based at the School of Scottish Studies at the University of Edinburgh who later went on to become Professor of Social Anthropology at Carleton University in Ottawa. The results of his work were published in an article entitled 'Burial and Mourning Customs in a Hebridean Community' in the *Journal of the Royal Anthropological Institute of Great Britain and Ireland* in 1955.

Vallee echoed Alexander Carmichael in emphasising the importance placed by the inhabitants of Barra, of whom he computed that 95 per cent were Roman Catholics, on 'a happy death' (see p. 106). 'The most important criterion of a happy death is the presence of a priest to bestow the last rites, the sacrament of extreme unction, during the last moments. Other criteria have a place, such as the absence of pain and the presence of loved ones at the bedside, but these are said to be of little consequence compared with the last rites, for it is the absolution of the priest which might prevent the departing soul from descending into hell.'[5]

This is a relatively rare mention of hell in the context of Hebridean and West Highland attitudes towards death. It is generally little referenced in sources after the time of Columba. In fact, Vallee notes later that, 'In no case that I know of was it assumed that the soul of a particular individual went to hell after death, no matter how evil his life in terms of the community *mores*. On the other hand, I have heard it said that a recently deceased person "must be in heaven; what a saint she was!"'.

The common assumption, he notes, was that 'at death, the soul of the departed is transported to purgatory where a period of expiation, immeasurable in terms of earthly time, must be undergone before the soul is brought to heaven'.[6] This emphasis on purgatory is, of course, exactly what one would expect to find in a strongly Roman Catholic community. It was from Barra that Carmichael had collected the song that speaks so eloquently of the cleansing that souls will go through in purgatory, where they will be 'fanned by the white wings of the fair angels of heaven' and become 'whiter than the swan of the songs, the seagull of the waves and the snow of the peaks' (p. 106).

As conceived by the Catholic population of Barra, purgatory had some similarities with that intermediate post-mortem state known as *bardo* in the Buddhist tradition. There are, of course, marked differences in belief between Catholics and Buddhists as to what ultimately follows death. For Buddhists, *bardo* is the period between one life and the next, an intermediate state in the cycle of reincarnation. The Catholic doctrine of purgatory suggests, rather, a period of cleansing and preparation to make the soul fit to enter heaven. But both states involve a kind of progression. In classic Tibetan Buddhism there are six stages of *bardo* in which the soul moves to greater detachment and enlightenment before its transmigration to another body. Purgatory is somewhat similarly conceived of by Catholics as a staged journey. Carmichael commented of the beliefs of Catholics in the Western Isles: 'There are four states, four places, in Purgatory, and the soul must pass through each one of these in turn. The soul is a forlorn sad little draggler, wet and cold, numbed with cold and rain, with snow and ice and sleet. And the soul is thus for ever until the priest wins it out and until a ransom is given for it.'[7]

Vallee was struck by the fact that the entire community was in some way affected by every death on the island, with very large numbers attending the funeral, except when the deceased was below five years of age, in which case a simple burial service was carried out attended by just the priest and close relatives. In all other cases, no organised recreational activities, such as dances, concerts and card parties, were held anywhere on the island during the period between a death and a burial. Those living near the home of the deceased generally abstained from working on the land or fishing while a body was 'lying in state' (in Gaelic *os cionn talamhainn*, literally 'above the ground').

> The largest share of responsibility for dealing with the crisis of death almost always falls on the closest adult able-bodied male relative of the deceased, whom we might refer to as the chief mourner. Shortly after the death it is customary for this person to repair to the public house to purchase spirits and beer. In the public bar he receives the condolences of other adult males. His appearance at the public house can be regarded as the initial 'public' act in the ritual sequence. It is understood that no matter how short the supply of whisky on hand, at least one bottle is made available to the household of death for the mourners. It is also the duty of the chief mourner to advise one of the island joiners of the death so that a coffin can be manufactured.[8]

In each township there were women who regularly washed and dressed the bodies of those who died. Unlike the joiner, who was paid in cash for making the coffin, they were not given any remuneration for their work, which was carried out in teams of up to four, although they were generously treated to food and drink in the house of death, where they usually ate together at a separate table. The death garments, consisting of a plain under-shirt and an ornately decorated outer garment resembling the ceremonial robes of a priest, were usually made by these women with material supplied by the bereaved family. A diamond-shaped hood was placed over the face. Thus dressed, the 'remains' (*corp* in Gaelic) were placed in the sitting room or in a bedroom. In some houses, all pictures, except religious ones, in the death room were removed or turned to the wall, mirrors and windows covered with sheets or curtains and all the clocks stopped. Vallee noted that this was a custom which many Barra residents regarded as alien to the island's traditions and only relatively recently introduced by incomers from other parts of Scotland. He went on to describe the arrangement of the corpse on its bier or stand: 'Among all Catholics a bowl of holy water is placed on the bier alongside the body; Catholic mourners dip the fingers of the right hand in this and make the sign of the cross before kneeling to pray. On the chest of the corpse is placed a small dish of salt, around which one or two sets of rosary beads are entwined. Tall candles in stands are placed around the bier; these are kept alight while the body is in the house.'[9]

Similar arrangements had once been widespread across the Highlands and Islands. In his description of practices in Morvern in the mid nineteenth century, Norman MacLeod noted that 'from the time of death till that of interment, the body is watched day and night. A plate of salt is always placed upon the breast. Candles are also frequently lighted around it. These are the remains of Roman Catholic customs.'[10] Various suggestions have been offered as to the significance of the dish of salt. It may have been there for its antiseptic and preservative properties to delay decomposition, to keep away evil spirits, or to cleanse the deceased from impurities. In some cases, a piece of peat was also placed on the breast of the corpse.

Vallee's research revealed just how seriously the vigil around the body was taken in mid twentieth-century Barra:

> Seldom is the body kept for more than two days in the house. Normally, after a night and a day, it is removed to the chapel at which the deceased worshipped, where it remains alone the night before burial. While the body is at the death-house a permanent vigil is kept. Most of the daytime visitors are female; males usually choose evening and night time for their visits. Group prayers are said periodically by the Catholic mourners. Each session of prayers is closed with a request that God assure the 'repose of this soul and the souls of all the faithful departed', whose company the deceased has presumably joined.

> Relatives up to the third degree of consanguinity and affines of the deceased are expected to make special efforts to pay their respects, as are all close friends and neighbours of the deceased and his elementary family. It is expected also that they will bring articles of food and refreshment to supplement the household stocks. No invitations are issued, either to visit or to attend the funeral.

> During the night the body is 'watched' by male relatives and friends and the closest adult female relatives. At least one of these persons, almost always male, maintains a vigil by the side of the body, while the others usually sit in the kitchen. It is not unusual for many men to arrive after closing time of the public house, carrying half-bottles of whisky and bottles of beer, to supplement the supply of liquor already procured by the chief mourner. Contrary to popular opinion in many parts of Britain, these wakes are not drunken parties. The men sit in the

kitchen discussing male topics – seamanship, fishing, sheep, etc., – taking turns in sitting beside the 'remains' for spells of a quarter-hour or so. The few women present are usually busy preparing snacks and cleaning up about the kitchen. There is no singing or 'keening'. On several occasions during the night watch, all move from the kitchen to the death room; there the Catholics kneel and pray aloud. No particular person is responsible for deciding when these periods of prayer are to occur, but it is always a close relative of the deceased, and usually the chief mourner, who leads the praying.

On the afternoon following the wake, usually at about 4 o'clock, relatives and friends in large numbers gather at the house for the ceremony of the 'lifting' (Gaelic *an togail*) the body into the coffin. The priest, or in his absence the chief mourner, leads the group in prayer as the coffin lid is closed over the body. At this point the manifestation of grief, especially on the part of women, is expected to reach a point only to be exceeded at the burial.

The closed coffin is placed on a rectangular board from both sides of which extend three shafts. Six men each grasp a shaft and bear the coffin in procession to the Chapel. Males lead the procession, walking in pairs, followed by the coffin, behind which walk the women.

A close friend or relative of the deceased assumes the role of procession-master, deciding the frequency and spacing of reliefs for the bearers of the coffin. Walking alongside the lines of men, he either blows a whistle or calls out when the coffin is to change hands. At his signal, the leading six men fall out of the procession, three on each side of the road, and wait there until the

coffin draws level with them, when they step forward
and relieve the carriers. The latter then attach themselves
to the rear of the procession. The staging of reliefs is
determined by the number of men present and the distance from house to chapel.

Immediately preceding the coffin walks the chief
mourner, normally the surviving male most closely
related to the deceased, holding a tassel at the end of a
white cord which is attached to the front of the coffin.
The closest female relative walks immediately behind
the coffin, holding a similar tassel.[11]

Vallee was struck by the egalitarian nature of the funeral procession, noting that 'it would not be considered remarkable if, for
example, the bank manager, a Protestant incomer of high social
status, walked at the side of an unemployed labourer, a cousin of
the deceased and a Catholic'.

On arrival at the chapel the procession is met by the
priest. The men bare their heads as he blesses the coffin
at the chapel door. Then all except leading members of
the Protestant congregation, who usually disperse at this
point, file into the chapel behind the coffin, which is
placed on a dais in front of the main altar. After a few
prayers the mourners depart, leaving the body in the
empty chapel until the Requiem Mass next morning.

After the Mass and prayers for the dead, the funeral
procession sets out for the cemetery. This procession is
identical with the one from home to chapel, except that
the funeral proper is attended by a greater number and
might be regarded as more of a total community event
than the procession from house to chapel.

In the procession, the only solemnity to be observed is in the immediate vicinity of the coffin among the bearers, tassel-holders, and the first rows of women. Beyond this area, people chat quietly about the weather or current events as they walk along. One of the few island pipers plays a lament during the funeral procession if the deceased is a relative or close friend of his, or a prominent personage. Should the procession pass non-participant bystanders, the latter are expected to stand still and bow their heads as the *cortège* goes by. It is not unusual for old women who are not in the procession to prostrate themselves at the roadside, their backs to the passing coffin.[12]

This last custom mentioned by Vallee may well have been a hangover from a tradition that Alexander Carmichael had noted in the 1870s:

> In Barra women leave the house along with the '*giùlan*', the body as it is carried, and go a certain distance. When they resolve to go no further they go upon their knees and pray, lifting the head now and then to look after the departing procession, and again intensifying their supplications and crossing themselves. The scene is striking, impressive, and picturesque —a woman here and a woman there and another a little beyond, in tartan gown and tartan '*guailleachan*', shoulder-plaid, fastened with a silver or a brass brooch, sometimes a tartan shawl over the head, or a high- crowned mutch.[13]

Although Barra still retained many traditions that had largely gone elsewhere, Vallee reported that even here things were changing. One example was the disappearance of keening. He also noted that 'until about twenty-five years ago it was customary for the procession to walk the entire distance from chapel to graveyard, but nowadays the greater part of the way is covered in motor cars and lorries'.[14] For most of the latter half of the twentieth century coffins were conveyed around Barra in the back of an ancient minibus, allowing close family members to travel with the deceased. The motorised hearse which Buchanan fervently hoped would not make an appearance until the last trump sounded did finally arrive on the island in the late 1990s. The practice of friends or neighbours digging the grave had ceased by the mid 1950s – this task was now performed by cemetery attendants paid by the District Council. These attendants also filled in the grave after the coffin had been lowered and relatives had thrown a handful of earth onto it. It was, however, still regarded as highly desirable to secure the first burial on a day when there was more than one interment, as the belief persisted that the last soul to be buried must guard the graveyard.

After the burial, mourners dispersed to the graves of their own relatives, where they knelt and prayed. Relatives of the deceased then returned to the death house to pay a 'comfort visit' and be entertained with liquor, tea, biscuits and cake. The tassels attached to the coffin during the processions to the chapel and burial ground, described as the 'family relic', were carefully stowed away in drawers along with other souvenirs of the deceased in the home of the chief mourner.

Vallee noted that there were no strict rules governing the wearing of mourning symbols and the length of mourning periods. Offspring of the deceased were expected not to attend concerts or dances for a year after the death, close adult male relatives usually wore a black tie for a few weeks and most widows wore mourning clothes for a few months. He was at pains to point out that 'this does not mean that the dead are quickly forgotten or that they cease to occupy a ritual status in the social structure'. For two years after death, the name of the deceased was spoken aloud by the priest during High Mass every Sunday in the chapel to which he or she belonged. Those speaking about the deceased would customarily follow mention of the name with 'some such pious ejaculation as "God rest him!"'. In private prayers the deceased might be asked to intercede on behalf of the living.

Seventy years on from Frank Vallee's study, Barra still retains several of the customs and practices that he noted, and that were once found throughout most of the Highlands and Islands. Many deaths still take place at home and it continues to be common for bodies, including of those who have died in hospitals and care homes, to remain in the family house for two days and nights while a constant vigil is kept over them. The wish to be brought home, from the mainland, to be buried among family and kin remains strong and the bodies of those born and brought up on the island are regularly brought over from the mainland on the CalMac ferry from Oban. However late the ferry arrives, there is always a group of friends and relations on the quayside ready to welcome them home.

Canon John Paul MacKinnon, Roman Catholic parish priest on the island of Barra, says that a 'good death' is still regarded as one where the priest is present to administer the 'last rites'. He notes that belief in purgatory has declined considerably and most people now think rather of the direct ascent of the departed soul to heaven. In some homes a window is left open in the room where the corpse is laid out to allow the soul to escape, especially when the priest is present at the moment of death. There is a general acceptance that the soul departs immediately and no sense of it lingering or hovering for a while. The practice of covering mirrors and pictures with a white cloth is still very common.

Female family members generally wash, prepare and dress the corpse, sometimes with the help of an experienced older woman from the township. Funeral garments are often prepared well in advance and stored in the linen cupboard. The diamond-shaped hood mentioned by Vallee is still used, but it is more common for the faces of the dead to be exposed and not covered over. A dish of salt is still placed on the breast of the corpse, often now with a pair of crossed rusty nails placed on top of it. This additional ritual, presumably designed to bring to mind the cross of Jesus, is, according to Canon MacKinnon, relatively recent and peculiar to Barra. On a table beside the corpse are two candlesticks, a crucifix and a bowl of holy water. Those visiting to pay their respects will either stand or kneel beside the corpse and they will dip their fingers into the bowl of holy water, make the sign of the cross upon themselves and then sprinkle some of the holy water over the body.

Canon MacKinnon says that throughout the two-day and night vigil someone will lead prayers – often the rosary – every two or three hours in the room where the deceased is laid out. At other times, those in the room will 'sit having their cups of tea with the deceased, tell stories and reminisce. It is not a mournful atmosphere. There will often be amusing and happy recollections which will raise a smile.' The body is usually taken from the home to the church the evening before the funeral service. Coffins are often carried into the graveyard and neighbours will split up into groups of six to share in carrying the coffin from the hearse to the grave, everyone in the local community having their opportunity to play a part in carrying the deceased to their final resting place. Although graves are dug by local council employees, it is not unknown for family members to join in the task. The priest is always present at the burial and he blesses the grave with holy water, leads the mourners in prayer and throws a handful of the

island's pure white sand onto the coffin. Then everyone around
the graveside comes forward to sprinkle some of the sand upon
the coffin too. In Canon MacKinnon's words, 'one moment
everyone is standing round the grave and then, after the final
prayer and blessing is said by the priest, the people disperse and
go off to different parts of the graveyard and kneel or stand in
prayer at the grave of a family member. No one rushes off to their
car – they will always pay their final respects at their own family
graves.' Following the burial, all the mourners return to the house
of the deceased for refreshments and a dram.

If a good number of the beliefs and customs surrounding death
and burial on Barra that Frank Vallee noted in the mid 1950s are
still there today, so too is the community spirit and support that
particularly impressed him. As Canon MacKinnon puts it, 'when
someone dies, it is as though a big arm goes round the island
and brings everyone together. First, a bottle of whisky arrives in
the house, then people arrive at the door with scones, pancakes,
sandwiches and a large pot of soup. The whole community ral-
lies round the mourners – everyone has their part to play in the
island community and no one is left out.'[15] His words echo the
conclusions that Frank Vallee drew from his study 70 years ago,
which are worth quoting in full for their moving and perceptive
assessment of the value of the Hebridean approach to death.

> To the Barraman death is not simply a sudden, arbitrary
> expulsion into a void. It is rather a major turning point
> in the human cycle. This view of death is evident in the
> way the series of activities are staged or phased. Indeed
> it is true to say that the passage from this world into the
> next begins some time before death itself occurs. Except
> in cases of sudden, unexpected death, the normal
> individual anticipates his departure and undergoes a

course of preparation for it, supported by the priest, his relatives, neighbours, and fellow members of his congregation. Nor does the actual moment of death signalize the complete exclusion of the deceased from his earthly milieu.

Firstly, there is the *os cionn talamhainn* while the body is at home and on display; then the period initiated by the rites of 'lifting' and closing the coffin, during which the body reposes in chapel; this is followed by the phase during which the recently deceased person, now below the soil, is mentioned by name each Sunday in chapel. With each step the dead person is farther removed from this world, although a tenuous connexion with the living is maintained, perhaps for generations, through prayer, the treasuring of mementoes, and the visiting of graves.

In contemplating his own demise, the Barraman is assured of ritual support both in preparation for death and in his passage from purgatory into heaven. Furthermore, he is assured of an indefinite extension of his social identity on earth. To the bereaved relatives, the widespread material and ritual support of the community comes at a critical time. The clearly defined series of rites provides them with socially accepted ways of adjusting to the difficult situation.

Mourning and burial rituals provide one of the most frequent occasions upon which community members meet to express their unity and to re-affirm the values upon which that unity is based. The average Barra adult, resident in the community, participates in from ten to fifteen wakes and funerals in a year. It is not surprising, therefore, that death in Barra is viewed as a familiar inherent part of the whole round of life, a 'normal' event. This view of death is evident in the way sacred and secular elements are unselfconsciously blended in the series of ritual. Mourning and burial are definitely 'religious' events: the priest is in attendance during the dying moments, he leads the rites at the 'lifting', receives the body at the chapel door, officiates at the funeral Mass and at the graveside; the appointments of the death room abound in religious connotations; group prayers and other religious gestures flow spontaneously from the mourners. Yet in the midst of these forms and acts of sanctity, mourners chat easily of ships and sheep and are concerned with ensuring that there is no shortage of liquor and food. Frequent attendance at these rites does more than breed familiarity with death; it intensifies the awareness of belonging to the community.[16]

Epilogue
Revisiting the Coffin Roads Today

This book has journeyed along the coffin roads and through the graveyards of the Highlands and Hebrides to explore attitudes and practices relating to death, dying, funerals and burials which are striking and distinctive. They integrate death into both the landscape and the culture, and make it something that is open and involves the whole community, rather than shut away and private. Death is seen very much as part of life, not trivialised but treated in a matter-of-fact way while at the same time being surrounded by ritual and envisaged as a journey to another state.

Much of what has been described in this book lies in the past and is now largely a matter of historical record. This is certainly true of the coffin roads themselves. No longer are coffins carried huge distances to graveyards by parties of bearers – hearses now do the job. The last funeral in the north of Skye in which a coffin was carried a considerable distance – in this case around two miles – took place in 1964. The practice of carrying coffins the last few hundred yards into churches and graveyards has lingered longest in the Western Isles. The coffin of Colin MacLeod, the Glasgow environmental and community activist who died at the age of 39 in 2005, was carried some considerable distance to his final resting place in Gravir, Lewis. The coffin of 14-year-old

Barra resident Eilidh Macleod, killed in the 2017 Manchester Arena bombing, was carried from the aircraft that brought her home across the island's main beach (the Tràigh Mhór) and later up the steep road to the church of Our Lady Star of the Sea in Castlebay by four family members at waist height, with other family members holding the traditional tassels at the front and back of the coffin and a piper leading the procession.

Burial remains the norm in the Highlands and Islands, unlike in other parts of Scotland and the United Kingdom, where most people are cremated. This is partly because there is still plenty of space and crematoria are a long way off (the only one in the entire region is in Inverness), but it also reflects the prevailing culture. However, even here things are changing. Canon John Paul MacKinnon says that increasingly he is laying to rest the cremated ashes, rather than the bodies, of those who have died on the mainland and wish to be brought back home to Barra.

Second sight and premonitions of death have not completely disappeared. In his book *Island Spirituality* Alastair McIntosh gives several recent examples. Norman Macleod, a retired policeman and lobster fisherman from Leverborough, Harris, had vivid premonitions of deaths before they occurred in the Falklands War in 1982, including seeing the warship HMS *Sheffield* 'with the metal superstructure going up in white incandescent flames'. McIntosh has also told me of an old man on Great Bernera who could locate the bodies of drowned fishermen because he heard their screams as they fell overboard, and a retired blacksmith on Lewis who saw a side road in the village of Leurbost full of cars a few days before an old woman died there. At her wake the scene was exactly as he had seen it.[1]

In these respects and in others Highlanders and Hebrideans have hung on to something that has largely disappeared in other places. Death has been swept under the carpet in most of

Scotland, as in the rest of the United Kingdom. It takes place out of sight behind screens in hospital wards or in discrete side rooms. The body is not taken home but rather to the mortuary or funeral parlour and then to the crematorium, where it is incinerated. The emphasis is on privacy, efficiency and cleanliness, with everything sanitised and left to the professionals. In the words of the British palliative care doctor and writer, Rachel Clarke:

> In today's developed world it is possible to live an entire lifetime without ever directly setting eyes on death, which, considering half a million Britons will die every year, is remarkable.
>
> Little more than a century ago, this distance from dying was inconceivable. We invariably departed the world as we entered it, among our families, close up and personal, wreathed not in hospital sheets but in the intimacy of our own homes. Now, though, both birth and death have become, by and large, institutionalized. The only two certainties around which our lives pivot have been outsourced to paid professionals.[2]

There is considerable evidence that this is not what people want. Recent polls suggest that 70 per cent of Scots would choose to die at home, yet at present only 25 per cent actually do so. In January 2020 David Stewart, a Labour MSP for the Highlands and Islands Region, initiated a debate in the Scottish Parliament in an attempt to establish an automatic right for people to have full care day or night for the last few days of their life, so enabling them to die at home. The debate was especially focused on the Highlands and Islands, and several speakers made references to traditions in those areas. David Stewart pointed out that the right to be born at home is enshrined in law but not the right to die there. Alasdair Allan, SNP MSP for Na h-Eileanan an Iar (the Western Isles) constituency, pointed out that 'dying is a taboo today in a way that it was not for earlier generations. Scottish literature is full of accounts of unabashedly matter-of-fact family arguments in front of, or including, elderly relatives about the catering arrangements that their family thinks are adequate for that person's funeral. Conversations as pragmatic as that would – perhaps not completely without reason – be considered fairly shocking today.'[3]

There are welcome indications that the taboo is finally being broken. In 2011 Jon Underwood set up the first death café in his home in Hackney, London, as a place where people could 'drink tea, eat cake and discuss death'. Ten years on, there were over 2,655 death cafés across the United Kingdom. There is a growing consensus that modern medicine has swung too far in striving to prolong life at all costs, focusing on its quantity rather than its quality. Dame Sue Black, the well-known Aberdeen-born pathologist, has lamented the fact that we have 'fallen out of love with death' and commended the Victorians' much more open and positive approach to it.[4] A clear majority of Scots, including a good number of those with religious convictions, support the principle of medical intervention to end the suffering experienced by some of those who are terminally ill, provided that there are adequate safeguards in place to avoid abuse and exploitation. The Assisted Dying for Terminally Ill Adults (Scotland) Bill was introduced in the Scottish Parliament by Liam McArthur, Liberal Democrat MSP for Orkney, in September 2021.

After more than a century when it has largely been off-limits, death is finally coming out of the closet and being discussed and faced much more openly. The coronavirus pandemic has played a significant role in bringing about this change of attitude. It has put death on the front pages of newspapers and into television news bulletins on a daily basis. It has also pushed up the death rate in Scotland: the number of people dying in 2021 was significantly higher – sometimes by as much as 500 per week – than in each of the previous three years. Quite apart from the effects of Covid, the death rate is increasing in Scotland thanks to the ageing of the population. It has been estimated that the number of annual deaths in the country will increase by 16 per cent from 2016 to 2040. Thanks to demographic factors, a disproportionate number of these deaths will be in the West Highlands and Hebrides. Argyll currently has the highest proportion of inhabitants over the age of 65 of any Scottish local government region (22 per cent compared to a national average of 17 per cent) and this is set to rise steeply over the coming years.

It is also highly likely that more people will die at home in the future. Between 2004 and 2016 the proportion of deaths taking place in hospitals declined by 8 per cent, with a corresponding rise in the proportion taking place at home and in care homes. If current trends continue, the number of deaths at home and in care homes will increase and two-thirds of deaths will occur outside hospitals by 2040. In 2016 in Scotland, 50 per cent of deaths occurred in hospitals, 23.4 per cent at home, 18.8 per cent in care homes and 4.3 per cent in hospices. By 2040 the proportion of those dying in hospital is predicted to fall to 34.3 per cent, deaths at home to rise to 29.4 per cent, in care homes to 29 per cent and in hospices to 4.7 per cent.[5]

In this respect we may perhaps be moving back closer to the situation that has long pertained in the Highlands. It would be good to think that this trend might lead to a revival of some of the attitudes and practices surrounding death that have been explored in this book. Yet even in the Catholic southern Outer Isles of Barra, Eriskay and South Uist where the traditions have lingered longest, there are signs of change. Father John Paul MacKinnon detects among younger people on Barra a desire to make the business of dying and death more clinical and removed and he fears that the old traditions of laying out corpses and maintaining a vigil over them in the home for two days and nights may only last for another 20 or 30 years.

There are some aspects of traditional Highland and Hebridean practice which are clearly not applicable to the mainland. The rise of cremations across the United Kingdom has been inexorable and seems certain to continue. They accounted for just 0.2 per cent of funerals in 1920. By 1970 the proportion was up to 42 per cent and in 2020 to 71 per cent. It is hard to see any reversal in this trend. The land for burials is just not available. Even as I write this, the front page of the Fife edition of *The Courier* reports that ten of Fife's cemeteries will be full by the end of this decade and that all of the region's graveyards will be full by the end of the century.[6] It is, of course, true that in increasingly opting for cremation we are returning to the practice of our prehistoric ancestors. The earliest burials in the Kilmartin Valley were of cremated remains rather than corpses.

The most pronounced trend in current funeral practices is towards direct cremation, where there is no service or ceremony and no mourners. In the first half of 2020, direct cremations accounted for 25 per cent of all funerals, and the proportion seems set to rise. Although the growth of this practice is largely driven by cost, it is also popular because it allows the bereaved to focus more on celebrating the life of the deceased and, in the words of respondents to a 2021 survey on 'The Cost of Dying' by the insurance company SunLife, to 'spend more money on the wake than the funeral'.[7] A 2019 report from the Co-op, which conducts more than 100,000 UK funerals a year, found that 21 per cent of people feel that 'the wake will actually become more important than the funeral service'.[8]

If there are going to be more deaths taking place at home and more emphasis on the wake and the commemoration of the deceased, some of the traditional customs and practices surrounding death and funerals in the Highlands and Hebrides may provide helpful pointers to making death feel less remote and frightening and easing the grieving process. Not least of these is the wake, which does seem to be coming back into prominence. In Lorn Macintyre's words, 'the wake was like a ceilidh. You gathered people round the open coffin and they told stories and jokes which composed a picture of the deceased. It linked the living and the dead and kept the departed alive in memory. It is still practised in some families. In my brother Kenny's coffin his two sons placed a mobile phone, and grief gave way to hilarity about him ringing from the next world to see what was doing in this one. It's become part of the joyous folklore of my dear brother.'[9]

The involvement of the community has been a striking feature of many of the funerals described in this book, as has the physical journey of the deceased through the local landscape. Many of the funerals that have taken place during the Covid lockdowns have involved taking the coffin on a journey round the local area, visiting significant places in the life of the deceased, such as home, workplace, favourite shop, pub or café, sports club, park or place of worship. People have come out along the route of these journeys to pay their respects rather as they did in the days of the coffin roads. Perhaps this relatively new trend will continue beyond the pandemic and we will see more community involvement in funerals.

It seems unlikely that we will go back to dressing and laying out corpses and keeping the body of the deceased in the house for a period of days and nights. However, given the expected rise in the number of deaths taking place at home and the increasing emphasis on wakes, there is surely a case for making the transition from life to death more gradual and marking it with rituals which can help the expression of grief and give it meaning and context. Such rituals are constantly changing, of course: there are relatively new ones like the bunches of flowers and other symbols which are left at the sites of fatal road accidents, murders and terrorist attacks. The Hebridean and Highland experience reminds us of their importance, whether new or old.

It may be worth revisiting some of the other specific traditions discussed in this book, such as the intoning over the terminally ill and dying of the soul peace or death croon with their message of going home and a calm and peaceful sleep. If more people are going to die at home there will be opportunities for family members, friends and others to help them on their final journey with song and poetry. It is well known that someone who is unconscious and in a coma can hear speech and song. John Bell, the leading contemporary hymnwriter and worship worker with the Iona Community, tells of how one of his clerical colleagues visited a man in a coma on the same day every week and always ended by reciting the 23rd psalm. In time the man recovered consciousness and spoke of how when in the coma he had looked forward particularly to the psalm being recited over him.[10] The role of music in palliative care is already well appreciated – I know of one musician who regularly goes into a hospice to play her harp to those who are dying. The idea of the Celtic *anamchara* or soul friend, which has already been rediscovered and promoted in contemporary pastoral care, may have important resonances in palliative end of life care and in facilitating a good death.

There may also be a case for reviving and encouraging the practice of keening and expressing grief through lament and song. I echo what Noel O'Donoghue has written about these traditional funeral songs: 'They do indeed mourn the dead and evoke a whole river of tears, but this mourning should open up a kind of pathos

.that is truly homeopathic. It heals the wounds of bereavement by touching these wounds in such a way that the funeral song of loss and departure opens up the hidden light within the memory of those same wounds: the heart of a man and woman in mourning is touched by a strange balm which only certain kinds of music and ceremonial can convey.'[11]

There is also much we can learn from the Highland and Hebridean emphasis on locating the dead in the physical landscape. This is obviously easier when they lie in graveyards and cemeteries, but the ashes from cremations are often taken and scattered in rivers, streams, woods and hedgerows, on the tops of hills and mountains, and along the seashore. In this way, we can make the connection between the living, the dead and the landscape and to help establish that sense of a continuing presence of those who have gone before, not in a spooky or ghoulish sense but in such a way as is conveyed in the 'Death Song of Ossian': 'The sons of song are gone to rest. My voice remains, like a blast, that roars, lonely, on a sea-surrounded rock, after the winds are laid. The dark moss whistles there; the distant mariner sees the waving trees!'[12]

At the heart of much of what I have written about in this book was a strong set of religious beliefs and a firm faith in the afterlife and in the doctrine of the communion of saints, with its conviction that only a thin veil separates us from those who have gone before and are now in the nearer presence of God and still with us in the mystery of the one family in heaven and earth. For many of those in the Highlands and Islands this was rooted in Christian conviction although, as we have observed, Christianity is not without its own ambiguities when it comes to what happens after death – is it a direct ascent to heaven (or descent to hell), a long sleep followed by a day of judgement, a general resurrection, or a period of cleansing and testing in purgatory? All three positions have been maintained by Church teachers and theologians. The

Highland and Hebridean approach to death, as to so many other matters, was an amalgam of Christian and primal pagan beliefs. As Elizabeth Grant of Rothiemurchus put it, 'our mountains were full of fairy legends, old clan tales, forebodings, prophecies, and other superstitions, quite as much believed in as the Bible. The Shorter Catechism and the fairy stories were mixed up together to form the innermost faith of the Highlander.'[13]

Today just over half the population of the United Kingdom believe in a continuing existence after death. A survey undertaken by Maru Public Opinion in April 2021 put the figure at 55 per cent and indicated, perhaps somewhat surprisingly, that belief in an afterlife is highest (64 per cent) among 18 to 24 year olds and lowest (37 per cent) among those over 65. There are many views about the nature of this existence, with a substantial minority favouring reincarnation and others seeing a future life in the stars, alongside more conventional Christian views of immortality and resurrection. Polls taken over the last decade consistently show that around a third of the population of the UK believe in angels (among women the proportion is 40 per cent, and among the general population in the USA it is over 70 per cent).[14] Perhaps those many references to angels in Highland and Hebridean stories and songs can speak to people today more than we might imagine, and help them to conquer the fear of death. In the words of George MacLeod, 'the cry should not be "back to the angels" but "forward to the angels" – how much do we not need them again? We must recover the ancient insight that all forces are ultimately personal, all motions ultimately directed in the service of love.'[15]

Some fascinating findings emerge from the 2019 Co-op report on the changing face of UK funerals. Based on substantial research and a YouGov poll, it reveals a mixed picture, with some traditional practices on the up and others in decline. There is clear evidence of rising interest in eco-friendly funerals using bio-degradable coffins, with almost a fifth of respondents expressing a preference for these. A similar proportion asked for objects to be put in their coffin, among the more unusual being a Chinese takeaway, a pork pie and a Toffee Crisp. If both these trends hark back to very early Celtic practices, there is clear evidence that in other respects we are moving away from long-established traditions. Perhaps the most dramatic is the drop in requests for traditional pallbearers to carry coffins, from 91 per cent of funerals in 2014 to 20 per cent in 2019.

The Co-op report does suggest that the subject of death is gradually becoming less of a taboo, although, extrapolating from the survey findings, it estimates that around 16.5 million people in the UK (nearly a quarter of the population) still feel uncomfortable talking about it. Its clearest finding is the rapid decline of the traditional religious funeral over the last decade. In 2011, 67 per cent of people requested traditional religious services and just 12 per cent were non-religious. By 2018, just 10 per cent wanted a religious funeral, an 80 per cent decline in less than a decade. Undertakers report a 'staggering shift' towards unique, secular ceremonies and a move to more informality and individuality.[16]

Even if we are seeing a significant shift to more secular and informal funerals, the customs and traditions described in this book may still offer helpful and consoling alternatives to the modern minimalist, utilitarian, clinical, professional approach to death which tends to deny and downplay it. We could do with being more open about it, giving people more space to grieve, just as we also need to give more support to the dying, not just through better palliative end of life care but through spiritual nourishment. We perhaps need to support the dead more, too. As Alastair McIntosh put it to me, reflecting on the story of the three Highland ladies and their death croon for the English soldier

(p. 99): 'perhaps we are neglecting the needs of the dead. We are failing to bake the bannock, light the lamp and fashion the key. We are failing as the communion of saints in our saintly duties.'[17]

Not all are guilty of this neglect, and I end this book with a modern hymn about death directly inspired by one of the coffin roads that have provided its overarching theme. The 'Iona Boat Song' is traditionally said to have been sung by those rowing bodies across the Sound of Iona prior to their final journey along the Street of the Dead to the Reilig Odhráin. Among those who have been inspired to set words to its tune have been John MacLeod, minister of Morvern from 1824 to 1882, Hugh Roberton, the founder of the Glasgow Orpheus Choir, and most recently, John Bell and the late Graham Maule of the Iona Community, who invoke angels and dreams to present death in an essentially positive light as a journey. In so doing, they seem to me to stand very much in the Highland and Hebridean tradition and at the same time to offer something contemporary and relevant today. This is how John Bell introduces the text, which is entitled 'The Last Journey': 'Legend has it that the tune of this song was played when the ancient kings of Scotland were ferried from the mainland to their resting place on the island of Iona. The text indicates how, in leaving the community of God's people on earth, we do not become lonely, forgotten souls, but are companioned by the perfect community of the three-personned God and the angels of heaven.'[18]

> From the falter of breath,
> through the silence of death,
> to the wonder that's breaking beyond;
> God has woven a way,
> unapparent by day,
> for all those of whom heaven is fond.

From frustration and pain,
through hope hard to sustain,
to the wholeness here promised, there known;
Christ has gone where we fear
and has vowed to be near
on the journey we make on our own.

From the dimming of light,
through the darkness of night,
to the glory of goodness above;
God the spirit is sent
to ensure heaven's intent
is embraced and completed in love.

From today till we die,
through all questioning why,
to the place from which time and tide flow;
angels tread on our dreams,
and magnificent themes
of heaven's promise are echoed below.[19]

Notes

Any websites listed were last accessed in January 2022, unless otherwise noted.

Introduction

1 Norman MacLeod, *Reminiscences of a Highland Parish* (London: Strahan & Co., 1871), pp. 231–2.

2 Osgood Mackenzie, *A Hundred Years in the Highlands* (London: Edward Arnold, 1921), pp. 200–1.

3 Ibid., pp. 204–7.

4 MacLeod, *Reminiscences of a Highland Parish*, p. 225.

5 A.E. Robertson, *Old Tracks: Cross-country Routes and 'Coffin Roads' in the North-west Highlands* (Edinburgh: Darien Press, 1941), p. 12.

6 John MacInnes, 'The Church and Traditional Belief in Gaelic Society', in Lizanne Henderson (ed.), *Fantastical Imaginations: The Supernatural in Scottish History and Culture* (Edinburgh: John Donald, 2009), p. 186.

7 Noel Dermot O'Donoghue, *The Mountain Behind the Mountain: Aspects of the Celtic Tradition* (Edinburgh: T & T Clark, 1993), p. 24.

8 Karl Rahner, *On the Theology of Death*, trans. C.H. Henkey (New York: Herder & Herder, 1961), p. 34.

1 Kilmartin Valley

1   Graham Ritchie (ed.), *The Archaeology of Argyll* (Edinburgh University Press, 1997), p. 67.

2   Rachel Butter, *Kilmartin: Scotland's Richest Prehistoric Landscape* (Kilmartin: Kilmartin House Trust, 1999), p. 80.

3   Isabel Grant, *Highland Folk Ways* (London: Routledge and Kegan Paul, 1961), p. 366

4   James Boswell, *Journal*, 21 October 1773, quoted in Ian Bradley, *Argyll: The Making of a Spiritual Landscape* (Edinburgh: St Andrew Press, 2015), pp. 14–15.

5   Charles John Shore, 2nd Baron Teignmouth, *Sketches of the Coasts and Islands of Scotland*, Vol. I (London: John W. Parker, 1836), p. 199.

6   Geddes MacGregor, *Images of Afterlife* (New York: Paragon House, 1992), p. 55.

7   David Lewis-Williams and David Pearce, *Inside the Neolithic Mind: Consciousness, Cosmos and the Realm of the Gods* (London: Thames and Hudson, 2005), p. 179.

8   Thomas Ratcliffe Barnett, *The Land of Lorne* (Edinburgh: Chambers, 1933), p. 64.

9   Ibid., pp. 11, 144.

2 The Street of the Dead, Iona

1   The route of the coffin road across Mull is described in more detail in Mary McGrigor, *Paths of the Pilgrims* (Dalkeith: Scottish Cultural Press, 2006), pp. 24–5.

2   Ewan Campbell and Adrián Maldonado, 'A New Jerusalem "At the Ends of the Earth": Interpreting Charles Thomas's Excavations at Iona Abbey 1956–63', *The Antiquaries Journal*, Vol. 100, (2020), pp. 52–3.

3   The text of the 'Altus Prosator' is to be found in Thomas Owen Clancy and Gilbert Márkus, *Iona: The Earliest Poetry of*

a Celtic Monastery (Edinburgh: Edinburgh University Press, 1995), pp. 48–53.

4   Adomnán, *Life of Columba*, trans. William Reeves (Edinburgh: Edmonston & Douglas, 1874), pp. 98–9.

5   Samuel Johnson, *A Journey to the Western Islands of Scotland* (London: Penguin Books, 1984), pp. 142–3. See also Martin Martin, *A Description of the Western Islands of Scotland circa 1695* (Edinburgh: Birlinn, 1994), p. 289.

6   James E. Fraser, *Iona and the Burial Places of the Kings of Alba* (University of Cambridge, 2016).

7   Campbell and Maldonado, 'A New Jerusalem', p. 65.

8   Alexander Carmichael, *Carmina Gadelica*, Vol. 2 (Edinburgh: Oliver & Boyd, 1928), p. 340.

9   G.R.D. McLean, *Poems of the Western Highlanders* (London: SPCK, 1961), p. xxxii.

3   Jura

1   Alexander Kennedy in *The New Statistical Account of Scotland*, Vol. VII, Renfrew & Argyle (Edinburgh: Blackwood, 1845), p. 535.

2   Aisling Byrne, *Otherworlds: Fantasy and History in Mediaeval Literature* (Oxford University Press, 2015), pp. 2, 10. See also the chapter by Elizabeth Boyle, 'The Afterlife in the Mediaeval Celtic Speaking World', in *Imagining the Medieval Afterlife*, Richard Pollard (ed.) (Cambridge University Press, 2020).

3   *The Voyage of Bran*, trans. Kuno Meyer (Cambridge, Ontario: In Parenthesis Publications, 2000), pp. 1–2.

4   Alastair McIntosh, *Poacher's Pilgrimage* (Edinburgh: Birlinn, 2018), p. 265.

5   John D. Anderson, 'The *Navigatio Brendani*: A Medieval Best Seller', *The Classical Journal*, Vol. 83 (1988), pp. 315–22.

6   Denis Donoghue (ed. and trans.), *Brendaniana: Brendan*

the *Voyager in Story and Legend* (Dublin: Browne & Nolan, 1893), p. 174.

7   Peter Youngson, *Jura Parish Church, 1777 to 1977* (Glenrothes: Dolphin Press, 1977), p. 17.

8   Charles John Shore, 2nd Baron Teignmouth, *Sketches of the Coasts and Islands of Scotland*, Vol. II (London: John W. Parker, 1836), pp. 347–50

9   Ibid., Vol. I, pp. 190–1.

10 Ibid., Vol. I, p. 183.

11 Elizabeth Grant, *Memoirs of a Highland Lady* (London: John Murray, 1898), p. 192.

12 Shore, 2nd Baron Teignmouth, *Sketches of the Coasts and Islands of Scotland*, Vol. I, pp. 183–7.

13 Ibid., p. 189.

14 Ibid., pp. 192–3.

15 Ibid., p. 197.

16 Ibid., p. 197.

17 Ibid., p. 196.

4   Morvern

1   The route is described in <http://www.heritagepaths.co.uk/pathdetails.php?path=70>.

2   Norman MacLeod, *Reminiscences of a Highland Parish* (London: Strahan & Co., 1871), pp. 223–5.

3   Ibid., pp. 241–4.

4   Ibid., p. 241.

5   Alexander Carmichael, *Carmina Gadelica*, Vol. 3 (Edinburgh: Oliver & Boyd, 1940), p. 370.

6   MacLeod, *Reminiscences of a Highland Parish*, p. 242.

7   Ibid., pp. 265–8.

8   Ibid., pp. 225–7.

9   Ibid., pp. 219–20.

5 The Green Isle, Loch Shiel

1   Norman MacLeod, *Reminiscences of a Highland Parish* (London: Strahan & Co., 1871), pp. 220–3.

2   Karen Ralls-MacLeod, *Music and the Celtic Otherworld* (Edinburgh: Polygon, 2000), p. 68.

3   For examples, see Ian Bradley (ed.), *The Quiet Haven: An Anthology of Readings on Death and Heaven* (London: Darton, Longman and Todd, 2021).

4   Alexander Ross, *Memoir of Alexander Ewing* (London: Daldy, Isbister & Co., 1877), p. 592.

5   Jehanne Wake, *Princess Louise: Queen Victoria's Unconventional Daughter* (London: Collins, 1988), p. 391, quoting a letter from Lorne to the Duchess of Argyll, 23 February 1868, in the Inveraray Mss.

6   Ian Bradley, *Argyll: The Making of a Spiritual Landscape* (Edinburgh: St Andrew Press, 2016), pp. 156, 238.

7   Mary Donaldson, *Further Wanderings – mainly in Argyll* (Paisley: Alexander Gardner, 1926), p. 304.

6 The Piper's Cairn, Eigg

1   Norman MacLeod, *Morvern: A Highland Parish*, ed. Iain Thornber (Edinburgh: Birlinn, 2012), p. 223; Charles John Shore, 2nd Baron Teignmouth, *Sketches of the Coasts and Islands of Scotland*, Vol. I (London: John W. Parker, 1836), pp. 192, 195.

2   Norman MacLeod, *Reminiscences of a Highland Parish* (London: Strahan & Co., 1871), p. 232.

3   Marjory Kennedy-Fraser and Kenneth Macleod, *Songs of the Hebrides* (London: Boosey, 1922), Vol. I, p. 104.

4   For further discussion of the role of the *anamchara*, see Ian Bradley *Colonies of Heaven: Celtic Models for Today's Church* (London: Darton, Longman and Todd, 2000), pp. 101–14.

5   Kennedy-Fraser and Macleod, *Songs of the Hebrides*, Vol. I,
    p. 98.
6   Ibid., p. 104.
7   Ibid., p. 104.
8   Ibid., p. 104.
9   Alastair McIntosh, *Poacher's Pilgrimage: An Island Journey*
    (Edinburgh: Birlinn, 2018), pp. 247–9.
10 Alexander Carmichael, *Carmina Gadelica* (Edinburgh: Floris
    Books, 1992), p. 578.
11 Ibid., p. 578.
12 Ibid., p. 312.
13 Ibid., p. 67.
14 Ibid., p. 253.
15 Ibid., p. 635.
16 Ibid., p. 310.
17 Ibid., p. 634.
18 Alexander Carmichael, *Carmina Gadelica*, Vol. 3 (Edinburgh:
    Oliver & Boyd, 1940), p. 371.
19 Ibid., p. 309.
20 Ibid., p. 634.
21 Noel O'Donoghue, *The Angels Keep Their Ancient Places*
    (Edinburgh: T & T Clark, 2001), p. 101.
22 Samuel Curkpatrick, 'Into the profound deep', in Helen Dell
    and Helen Hickey, *Singing Death: Reflections on Music and
    Mortality* (Abingdon: Routledge, 2017), p. 28.
23 Mary McLaughlin, 'Moving between worlds: death, the other
    world and traditional Irish song', in Dell and Hickey, *Singing
    Death*, pp. 108, 115.
24 John Purser: *Scotland's Music* (Edinburgh: Mainstream
    Publishing, 1992), p. 24.
25 Ibid., pp. 24, 25.
26 Charles John Shore, 2nd Baron Teignmouth, *Sketches of
    the Coasts and Islands of Scotland*, Vol. I (London: John W.
    Parker, 1836), p. 195.

27 Alexander Carmichael, *Carmina Gadelica*, Vol. 5 (Edinburgh: Oliver & Boyd, 1954), p. 339.

28 Ibid., p. 338.

29 Ibid., pp. 344–5.

30 Alexander Carmichael, *Carmina Gadelica* (Edinburgh: Floris Books, 1992), p. 575.

31 Ibid., p. 635.

32 *Oban Times*, 11 June 1912.

33 *Songs of the Hebrides*, Vol. 1, p. xxxvii.

7 Kintail

1 A.E. Robertson, *Old Tracks: Cross-country Routes and 'Coffin Roads' in the North-west Highlands* (Edinburgh: Darien Press, 1941), p. 8.

2 Iain Thomson, *Isolation Shepherd* (Inverness: Bidean Books, 1983), p. 115.

3 Frank Smythe, *The Mountain Vision* (London: Hodder & Stoughton, 1941), pp. 109–10.

4 John Lorne Campbell and Derick Thomson, *Edward Lhuyd in the Scottish Highlands* (Oxford: Clarendon Press, 1963), p. 54.

5 Martin Martin, *A Description of the Western Islands of Scotland* (Edinburgh: Birlinn, 1994), p. 321.

6 Ibid., pp. 326, 334–5, 339–40.

7 Ibid., pp. 327–8.

8 Norman MacLeod, *Reminiscences of a Highland Parish* (London: Strahan & Co., 1871), p. 228.

9 John Gregorson Campbell, *The Gaelic Otherworld*, ed. Ronald Black (Edinburgh: Birlinn, 2005), p. 235.

10 Ibid., pp. 254–5.

11 Ibid., p. 255.

12 Ibid., p. 263.

13 Ibid., p. 265.

14 Charles John Shore, 2nd Baron Teignmouth, *Sketches of the Coasts and Islands of Scotland*, Vol. I (London: John W. Parker, 1836), p. 196.

15 Letter to Lord Bute, 8 August 1894, quoted in John Lorne Campbell and Trevor Hall, *Strange Things* (London: Routledge & Kegan Paul, London, 1968), p. 57.

16 *Strange Things*, p. 282.

17 Ibid., p. 292.

18 *Tales from Barra Told by the Coddy* (Edinburgh: Birlinn, 1992), p. 123.

19 Ibid., p. 127.

20 John Gregorson Campbell, *The Gaelic Otherworld*, ed. Ronald Black (Edinburgh: Birlinn, 2005), p. 240.

21 Anne Ross, *The Folklore of the Scottish Highlands* (London: Batsford, 1976), pp. 42–3.

22 Lorn Macintyre, conversation with the author, 30 November 2021.

23 Shore, 2nd Baron Teignmouth, *Sketches of the Coasts and Islands of Scotland*, Vol. I, p. 192.

24 MacLeod, *Reminiscences of a Highland Parish*, p. 228.

25 Ibid., p. 231.

26 Thomas Ratcliffe Barnett, *The Land of Lochiel and the Magic West* (Edinburgh: Robert Grant & Son, 1927), p. 39.

8   Barra

1   Thomas Ratcliffe Barnett, *The Road to Rannoch and the Summer Isles* (Edinburgh: Robert Grant & Son, 1924), pp. 8–9.

2   Donald Buchanan, *Reflections of the Isle of Barra* (London: The Catholic Book Club, 1942), pp. 126–7.

3   Ibid., p. 116.

4   Ibid., p. 117.

5   F.G. Vallee, 'Burial and Mourning Customs in a Hebridean
    Community', *The Journal of the Royal Anthropological Institute
    of Great Britain and Ireland*, Vol. 85, No. 1/2 (1955), p. 121.

6   Ibid., p. 121.

7   Alexander Carmichael, *Carmina Gadelica*, Vol. 3 (Edinburgh:
    Oliver & Boyd, 1940), p. 370.

8   Vallee, 'Burial and Mourning Customs', p. 122.

9   Ibid., p. 123.

10 Norman MacLeod, *Reminiscences of a Highland Parish*
    (London: Strahan & Co., 1871), p. 231.

11 Vallee, 'Burial and Mourning Customs', pp. 123–4.

12 Ibid., p. 125.

13 Alexander Carmichael, *Carmina Gadelica*, Vol. 3 (Edinburgh:
    Oliver & Boyd, 1940), p. 370.

14 Vallee, 'Burial and Mourning Customs', p. 125.

15 Canon John Paul MacKinnon, telephone interview with
    author, 23 November 2021.

16 Vallee, 'Burial and Mourning Customs', pp. 127–8.

Epilogue

1   Alastair McIntosh, *Island Spirituality* (South Lochs, Isle of
    Lewis: Islands Book Trust, 2013), pp. 83–4; email to author 19
    October 2021.

2   Rachel Clarke, 'What If Medicine is Not About Preserving
    Life, But About Humanity?', *Literary Hub*, 9 September 2020.

3   Verbatim report of debate in the Scottish Parliament, 29
    January 2020, on Right to Full Care to Die at Home, acces-
    sible via the website <https://www.theyworkforyou.com>

4   *The Times*, 26 September 2020.

5   These statistics are from Anne Finucane et al., 'The Impact of
    Population Ageing on End-of-Life Care in Scotland', *BMC
    Palliative Care*, Vol. 18, p. 112 (2019).

6   *The Courier*, Fife edition, 3 November 2021, pp. 1, 5.

7   'The Cost of Dying' report by SunLife, May 2021. Available online at <https://www.sunlife.co.uk/siteassets/documents/cost-of-dying/cost-of-dying-report-2021.pdf/>.

8   Co-op Media, 'Burying Traditions: The Changing Face of UK Funerals' (Co-op Media Report, 2019), p. 4. Available online via <https://www.coop.co.uk/funeralcare/funeral-trends>.

9   Lorn Macintyre, conversation with author, 30 November 2021.

10   John Bell, 'Celtic Perspectives on Death & Dying – Part 2', *GOOSEgander* 40 (Glasgow: Wild Goose Resource Group, Spring 2018), p. 11.

11   Noel O'Donoghue, *The Angels Keep Their Ancient Places* (Edinburgh: T & T Clark, 2001), pp. 42–3.

12   Elizabeth Sharp, *Lyra Celtica* (Edinburgh: Patrick Geddes, 1896), p. 41.

13   Elizabeth Grant, *Memoirs of a Highland Lady* (London: John Murray, 1898), p.212.

14   Bible Society poll December 2016. Available online at <https://www.biblesociety.org.uk/latest/news/a-third-of-all-brits-believe-in-guardian-angels>.

15   Ron Ferguson (ed.), *Daily Readings with George MacLeod* (London: Fount, 1991), p. 81.

16   Co-op Media, 'Burying Traditions', pp. 3, 11, 17.

17   Alastair McIntosh, email to author, 2 October 2021.

18   John Bell, *The Last Journey* (Glasgow: Wild Goose Resource Group, 1996), p. 22.

19   Ibid., p. 23.

Further Reading

Bradley, Ian, *Argyll: The Making of a Spiritual Landscape* (Edinburgh: St Andrew Press, 2016)

Bradley, Ian, *The Quiet Haven: An Anthology of Readings on Death and Heaven* (London: Darton, Longman and Todd, 2021)

Campbell, Ewan and Adrián Maldonado, 'A New Jerusalem "At the Ends of the Earth": Interpreting Charles Thomas's Excavations at Iona Abbey 1956–63', *The Antiquaries Journal*, Vol. 100, 2020 (London: Society of Antiquaries, 2020), pp. 374–407

Campbell, John Gregorson, *The Gaelic Otherworld*, ed. Ronald Black (Edinburgh: Birlinn, 2005)

Campbell, John Lorne and Trevor Hall, *Strange Things* (London: Routledge & Kegan Paul, 1968)

Carmichael, Alexander, *Carmina Gadelica* (Edinburgh: Floris Books, 1992)

Grant, Isabel, *Highland Folk Ways* (London: Routledge and Kegan Paul, 1961)

Kennedy-Fraser, Marjory and Kenneth Macleod, *Songs of the Hebrides* (London: Boosey, 1922)

Martin, Martin, *A Description of the Western Islands of Scotland* (Edinburgh: Birlinn, 1994)

McGrigor, Mary, *Paths of the Pilgrims* (Dalkeith: Scottish Cultural Press, 2006).

McIntosh, Alastair, *Island Spirituality* (South Lochs, Isle of Lewis: Islands Book Trust, 2013)

McIntosh, Alastair, *Poacher's Pilgrimage* (Edinburgh: Birlinn, 2018)

MacLeod, Norman, *Morvern: A Highland Parish*, ed. Iain Thornber (Edinburgh: Birlinn, 2012)

May, Peter, *Coffin Road* (London: Riverrun, 2016)

O'Donoghue, Noel Dermot, *The Mountain Behind the Mountain: Aspects of the Celtic Tradition* (Edinburgh: T & T Clark, 1993)

O'Donoghue, Noel, *The Angels Keep Their Ancient Places* (Edinburgh: T & T Clark, 2001)

Robertson, A.E., *Old Tracks: Cross-country Routes and 'Coffin Roads' in the North-west Highlands* (Edinburgh: Darien Press, 1941)

Ross, Anne, *The Folklore of the Scottish Highlands* (London: Batsford, 1976)

Teignmouth, Charles John Shore, 2nd Baron, *Sketches of the Coasts and Islands of Scotland*, Vols I, II (London: John W. Parker, 1836)

Vallee, F.G., 'Burial and Mourning Customs in a Hebridean Community', *The Journal of the Royal Anthropological Institute of Great Britain and Ireland*, Vol. 85, No. 1/2 (1955), pp. 119–30

Index